DIAPHANY
A JOURNAL & NOCTURNE

DIAPHANY
A Journal & Nocturne

Volume One

Edited by

AARON CHEAK, PHD
SABRINA DALLA VALLE, MFA
JENNIFER ZAHRT, PHD

RUBEDO PRESS
AUCKLAND · SEATTLE
2015

© Rubedo Press 2015

All rights reserved. No part of this work may be reproduced without express permission from the publisher. Brief passages may be cited by way of criticism, scholarship, or review, as long as full acknowledgement is given. All individual chapter authors and contributing artists retain copyright for their respective work, unless otherwise stated or arranged with the publisher.

Diaphany: A Journal & Nocturne
Edited by Aaron Cheak,
Sabrina Dalla Valle,
and Jennifer Zahrt

Published by Rubedo Press
www.rubedo.press
733 7th Ave, #107
Kirkland, WA 98033

ISSN: 2379-5190 (series)
ISBN: 978-1-943710-01-0 (volume)

Design and typography
by Aaron Cheak

Front and back cover images are light sensitive crystallisations photographed by Sabrina Dalla Valle, used with permission. All other images have been drawn from the public domain unless otherwise specified; full illustration credits are listed at the end of this volume.

'Beauty, Desire, and the Soul of the World' is reproduced with the kind permission of David Fideler and Inner Traditions International, from *Restoring the Soul of the World* (Rochester, Vermont: Inner Traditions, 2015). 'The Place of Nothing' is a modified version of chapter 10 of John W M Krummel's *Place of Dialectic, Dialectic of Place: Nishida Kitarō and Chiasmatic Chorology* (Bloomington: Indiana University Press, 2015). 'The Alchemical Chiasmus' is a revised version of a chapter originally appearing in Aaron Cheak, ed., *Alchemical Traditions: From Antiquity to the Avant-Garde* (Melbourne: Numen, 2013).

Peer-Review & Advisory

Ian Mills, PhD
Literary Theory (Film)
Emeritus, La Trobe University
Bundoora, Victoria, Australia

David Gordon White, PhD
History of Religions
University of California
Santa Barbara, California, USA

Eric Weiss, PhD
Philosophy, Cosmology, and
Consciousness; Esalen Center
for Theory and Research
Big Sur, California, USA

Rod Blackhirst, PhD
Philosophy and Religious Studies
La Trobe University
Bendigo, Victoria, Australia

Jennifer Lilla, PhD
Psychology, Imaginal Works
Portland, Oregon, USA

Anita Strezova, PhD
Art History, Theology,
Ancient History
Sydney, NSW, Australia

Rick Muller, PhD
Corporate Communications
Regis University
Denver, Colorado, USA

Gertrude Hughes, PhD
English Language and Literature
Emerita, Wesleyan University
Middletown, Connecticut, USA

Debashish Banerji, PhD
Indian Art History
Dean of Academic Affairs, University
of Philosophical Research
Los Angeles, California, USA

Nicole Keating, PhD
Chair of Communication
Woodbury University
Los Angeles, California, USA

Zephyros Kafkalides, LLD
Presocratic Philosophy
Corfu, Greece

Leon Marvell, PhD
Film and Digital Media
Deakin University
Melbourne, Victoria, Australia

Contents

Preface   11
    AARON CHEAK

Sensitive Crystallizations
    SABRINA DALLA VALLE   15

Rendering Darkness and Light Present: 21
Jean Gebser and the Prinicple of Diaphany
    AARON CHEAK

Never Paint what Cannot be Painted: 39
Master Dōgen and the Zen of the Brush
    JASON M WIRTH

Beauty, Desire, and the Soul of the World   67
    DAVID FIDELER

Arcane Cartographies: 95
An Interview with Timothy Ely
    SABRINA DALLA VALLE
    & TIMOTHY C ELY

Exploring the Fractal Nature of Ibn 'Arabī's Cosmology   115
    MOSELLE N SINGH

Never Born, Never Die: 141
Individuation, Mutation & Mystical Birth via
Gebser's Ever-Present Origin
    NICOLA MASCIANDARO

The Philosophy of the Flowers: 171
In Search for the Genealogy of Yūgen—A Cosmic Sublime
    ELISABET YANAGISAWA

The 'Place of Nothing' in Nishida as Chiasma and Chōra   203
    JOHN W M KRUMMEL

The Alchemical Chiasmus: 245
Creativity, Counter-Stretched Harmony, & Divine Self-Perception
    AARON CHEAK &
    SABRINA DALLA VALLE

Contributors   261

Illustration Credits   267

Nel suo profondo vidi che s'interna,
legato con amore in un volume,
ciò che per l'universo si squaderna.

In its depths I saw in-gathered,
and bound by Love into one volume,
all things that are scattered through the universe.

DANTE, *Paradisio* XXXIII, 85–87

Preface

¶ DIAPHANY is an international peer-reviewed volume dedicated to the living confluence of poetic, phenomenological, and empirical perceptions of reality. Drinking deeply from both the arts and the sciences, and then dissolving their boundaries, *Diaphany* weds the vital, experiential dimension of reality to rigorous, source-based research. By embracing the principle of qualitative presence, *Diaphany* seeks to breathe life into the academic *logos* in a way that infuses philosophical gravitas with a sweeping, visionary leaven.

The concept of diaphany is drawn from the work of German poet and *Kulturphilosoph*, Jean Gebser. For Gebser, transparency (*Durchsichtigkeit*) is that which renders both darkness and light present. *Diaphany* is designed accordingly as both a *journal* (from French *jour*, 'day') and a *nocturne*—a hymn to the night. Diaphany thus conceived is a matrix not only for the rational structures of consciousness (wakeful *logos* and light) but also for the pre-rational structures of consciousness (myth, dream, darkness).

Drawing on the romantic, integral, and phenomenological traditions in European philosophy, we use the word diaphany to evoke the process by which the nature of the whole shines through its parts; how, like the facets of a diamond, phenomenal surfaces are revealed as unique, living expressions of the deeper, holarchical reality from which they draw their life.

While strictly peer-reviewed, and while upholding the highest standards of academic research—including an unwavering fidelity to source materials—*Diaphany* is not a conventional academic journal. That is, *Diaphany* is not interested in so-called 'objective', 'dispassionate', or 'impersonal' inquiry for its own sake. Rather, *Diaphany* seeks work that is tempered in the fires of genuine wisdom rather than mere information; work that unveils the metaphysics of beauty through nondualistic perception; and work that emerges as much from a fervent, personal quest as it does from the perception of inexorable, impersonal realities.

Above all, *Diaphany* seeks to dissolve the artifical boundaries between philosophy, science, and art. It seeks philosophers in the strict sense—lovers of wisdom (*sophia*) whose work does not end in criticism for the sake of criticism, but in cultivating the life of the *psychē* in preparation for death (*meletē thanaou*); scientists sensitive to the Goethean ideal of 'delicate empiricism' (*zarte Empirie*), in which the harmonic structures of the cosmos are both poetically and pragmatically revealed; and artists of *poēsis* and presence who make the invisible visible and the eternal tangible according to a Kandinskian 'inner necessity' (*innere Notwendigkeit*).

AARON CHEAK

Sensitive Crystallizations

SABRINA DALLA VALLE

Inside and outside have become inadequate concepts.
—JACQUES LUSSEYRAN

¶ MANY YEARS AGO in the context of biodynamic gardening, I spent a lot of time wondering how the whole could reflect itself in the parts. Conversely, how could a plant indicate a greater picture of its surrounding? And more specifically, could individual plant species have consistent energetic vitality patterns that could somehow be evidenced? To answer this last question, I decided to experiment. I knew that salts were used in some types of chemical processes to record the footpaths left behind by the movement of energy forms. I had come across Dr Ehrenfried Pfeiffer's use of salts in blood samples to make medical diagnostics. These tests saturated salt crystals with blood in Petri dishes, which were then dehydrated under a specific temperature. Healthy blood samples were tested against unhealthy ones, and consistent appearance of deviant patterns revealed particular abnormalities in a person's health condition.

The most important principle for my purposes was that despite a constant incubation temperature, there exists a warmth variable in the dehydration of water that encourages salt to configure itself into crystallized forms—and warmth is a consequence of energy; we can call it 'heat energy'. Although we understand energy to be contained in our known universe as continuous and constant, having no beginning and no end, but rather transforming from one state to another, as energy moves between different states of matter, its movement is spurred by warmth. This 'heat energy' is more limited and can only be transferred from one body to a cooler body—and can be measured.

So, how can warmth be a signal of particular plant characteristics? In a two-year study done by Dr Paolo Carini and Dr Arthur Zajonc, warmth was observed through computer tabulations as the leading force in the growth of salt crystal forms in Petri dishes. Each crystal needle was created by an increase in temperature at a specific point in the dish. The more fern-like forms were indications of slow growth and the sharper star-like needles indicated fast growth. All salt samples were kept in incubators to maintain constant external temperature. Somehow the impurities in the substances that were tested fluctuated their own internal temperature while reacting with the salt. As the solution evaporated, it created a pattern of movement influenced by saturation levels evidenced in the remaining dry crystalline forms.

I decided to adapt this study to plant decoctions, making a 'tea' from different herbs that I grew in my garden. These samples almost invariably came forth with repeated and distinct crystal growth structures for each herb. I considered that each herbal decoction crystal growth was an archetype that pictured the movement of energy in a more general force field that is somehow responsible for the regulation of warmth and form for the plant in question. Knowing what to look for in these bursts of pattern would help to understand what they signified. I paid attention to the general aspect of the whole picture in each dish: regularity of the pattern, clarity of central and peripheral lines, characteristic and reproducible changes, changes in rim zone (widened, washed-out or stepped rim indicating lowered vitality in blood samples in Pfeiffer's work), course or fine needle thickness, and dense or loose density of stratification.

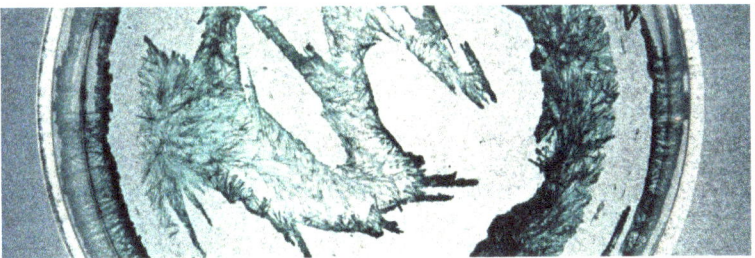

I feel these patterns of warmth energy speak a language similar to the language of blood samples interpreted by Dr Pfeiffer. Moreover, a deeper understanding of warmth energy can bring us closer to fundamental principles in awareness initiated by the early Greek Presocratics. At the time, the common theme worth documenting as text was 'On Nature'—both the inner human and outer natural world. Already in the sixth century BCE, there was a recorded sensitivity for transparency between the most introspective and external observations, a sense for two different expressions of a fundamental, life-sustaining dynamic.

My editorial work with *Diaphany* in this four-year journey of hunting, gathering, and preparation to launch our first issue is led by such desire to discover—and perhaps even experiment with—authentic altermodern voices that challenge the nature of this transparency to reveal something new about our current reality. Can we take nude risks and think in a different dimension about ourselves caught in the crossfire between values of medieval idealism and modern empiricism? This alphabet of experience/experiment is chaotic—but I feel we can serve as fulcrums teetering between subjectivity and distance in the way love (warmth) passes through trivial attraction and, just at the right moment, slides behind the veil of greater unseen life dimensions.

PAUL KLEE, *Growth of the night plants*, 1922.

Rendering Darkness and Light Present
Jean Gebser and the Principle of Diaphany

AARON CHEAK

> *More and more I am beginning to see behind or better: through things.*[1]
> —FRANZ MARC

> *What is innerness, if not intensified sky?*[2]
> —RAINER MARIA RILKE

¶ JEAN GEBSER (1905–1973) was a German poet, philosopher, and phenomenologist of consciousness. He is best known for his magisterial opus, *The Ever-Present Origin* (*Ursprung und Gegenwart*, 1949–1953), in which he articulates the structures and mutations of consciousness underpinning the pivotal shifts in human civilisation. Gebser's key insight was that as consciousness mutates toward its innate integrality, it drastically restructures human ontology and with it civilisation as a whole. Five hundred years before Christ, the fundamental mode of reality-perception mutated from *mythos* to *logos* through the agency of figures such as

---

1 *Franz Marc: Briefe, Schriften, Aufzeichnungen* (Leipzig: Gustav Kiepenheuer, 1989), 123. All translations are my own unless otherwise indicated.
2 Rilke, 'Oh, nicht getrennt sein…', Paris, Summer, 1925; *Rilke's Late Poetry*, trans. Graham Good (Vancouver: Ronsdale, 2004), 145.

Socrates, Siddhartha, and Lao Tzu. For Gebser, we are on the cusp of a new mutation, presaged by figures such as Rainer Maria Rilke, who in Gebser's view passed through 'things' into the transparent lucidity 'behind' things, thus breaking through to a new, aperspectival perception of reality.

The emphasis on diaphany (transparency) arises for Gebser from the perception that the nature of origin (*Ursprung*) is neither a primordial light nor a primordial darkness but a Diaphainon—that which 'renders darkness as well as brightness transparent or diaphanous'.[3] Diaphany, for Gebser, is a matrix for the rational structures of consciousness (wakeful *logos* and *light*) as well as the pre-rational structures of consciousness (myth, dream, darkness). Like the Upanishadic concept of *turiya* (the 'fourth' consciousness that lies at the root of all sleeping, dreaming, and waking) diaphany enables a deep openness to the archaic and nocturnal modes of being—the underworld and the unconscious—as equally as it does the light of day. In a letter to Georg Feuerstein, Gebser writes:

> I have never brought the 'dark' quality of the archaic consciousness into connection with a darkness of Origin. The archaic consciousness is only dark insofar as it 'lies' before the sleep-consciousness; Origin itself is transparent, unbound to darkness or brightness, which are simply attributes of manifestation.[4]

---

3 Jean Gebser, *Ursprung und Gegenwart*, Zweiter Teil, in *Gesamtausgabe*, III, 536: '[D]as Diaphainon aber, das Durchscheinende [...] Dunkel und Helligkeit transparent, diaphan, werden läßt'; *The Ever-Present Origin*, trans. Barstad and Mickunas (Athens, Ohio: Ohio University Press, 1985), 399.

4 Jean Gebser to Georg Feuerstein, 07-09-1972 (Schweizerishes Literaturarchiv, Bern): 'Ich habe nie das "Dunkle" des archaischen Bewusstseins mit einer

The word diaphany, like the word phenomenology, is based on the Greek verb *phainomai* (φαινομαι, 'to appear, shine'). Whereas phenomenology is the study of pure appearances as they manifest to consciousness, diaphany is concerned with that which appears or shines *through* phenomena (*dia*, 'through', + *phainomai*). Gebser refers to it variously as the *Durchscheinende* (the 'shining-through'), as *durchsichtig* ('transparent', 'see-through', 'invisible'), and as *hindurchscheint* (transluminated). Rather than delineating a 'world-view' (*Weltanschauung*) diaphany is, more specifically, a 'view *through* the world' (*Welt-durch-anschauung*).[5]

Now, the view *through* the world reveals the *roots* of the world. It is not simply the ability to see through material things as if they were made of glass. Rather, it is the ability to 'render present everything "behind" and "before" the world', and through this, 'to render present our own origin'.[6] What shines through (*dia*, *durch*) is no less than origin itself—the primordial leap (*Ur-Sprung*) made present through diaphanous perception. Significantly, such a mode of perception does not neglect the phenomenal world. It *fathoms* it. As Paul Klee remarks: 'Nature is not at the surface but in the depths. Colours are an expression of this depth at the surface. They

---

Dunkelheit des Ursprungs in Verbindung gebracht. Das archaische Bewusstsein ist nur insofern dunkel, als es noch vor dem Schlafbewusstsein "liegt"; der Ursprung selber ist transparent, umgebunden an dunkel oder hell, die blosse Manifestations-attribute sind'.
5 Gebser, 'Die Probleme in der Kunst', in *Gesamtausgabe*, V/1, 141. Here Gebser is drawing on Expressionist Franz Marc, one of the founders of the journal and movement, *Der Blaue Reiter*; in place of *Weltanschauung*, Marc suggests a *Welt-durchschauung*—i.e., a view *through* the world rather than a view *of* the world.
6 Gebser, *The Ever-Present Origin*, trans. Barstad and Mickunas, 7.

surge up from the roots of the world'.⁷

In a similar vein, this study seeks to explore the idea of diaphany not by examining Gebser's philosophical articulation of it—its surface—but by looking at the vital experiences that underpinned it—its depths. Rather than a purely conceptual approach, which risks mere abstraction, I have chosen to explore the principle of diaphany through Gebser's life experiences, through his poetic perceptions, and in particular, through his relationship to the work of Rainer Maria Rilke (1875–1926). To do this, there is perhaps no better starting point than the lightning-like flash of inspiration that, according to Gebser himself, seeded his entire life's work.

THE INTIMATE SKY

It was in Andalusia. Three years previously, in a spirit of primordial trust, he had abandoned both his fatherland and his mother-tongue in order to 'swim freely abroad in the foreign world'.⁸ Making his way through the South of France—Avignon, Aix-en-Provence, St-Jean-de-Gard—Gebser entered Spain in September 1929. By the winter of 1932–33 he found himself in the Spanish province of Málaga, near the southernmost periphery of Europe. It was here that he had what he later called the 'lightning-like inspiration' (*blitzartige Eingebung*) for his work on consciousness.⁹

---

7 Werner Haftman, *Paul Klee*, 1950, 87; cited in Gebser, *The Ever-Present Origin*, 516 n 167; and *Gesamtausgabe* V/1, 141.

8 Gebser, 'Die schlafenden Jahre', in *Gesamtausgabe*, VII, 363.

9 Gebser, *Verfall und Teilhabe*, in *Gesamtausgabe*, V/2: 'For the record: my concept of the development of a new consciousness, which came to my awareness in the winter of 1932/33 in a lightning-like flash of inspiration, and which I began to present since 1939, has extensive similarities to the world-design of Sri Aurobin-

Málaga, it should be noted, is one of the most ancient, continuously inhabited cities in the world. Founded by the Phoenicians almost three millennia ago, it has seen successive rule by Carthaginian, Roman, Byzantine, Arabic, and Spanish civilisations. As a consequence, the old-town is a veritable 'open museum' of this rich and deep heritage, and it is highly significant that Gebser's inspiration for the ever-presence of origin occurred in a city so visibly open to the presence of the past.

While Gebser does not describe the flash of inspiration specifically, if we look to the texts from this period, which are primarily in the form of poems and notebook entries, as well as his first monograph proper, *Rilke and Spain* (*Rilke und Spanien*, 1936/1944), which was first prepared for publication in Madrid, we gain some distinct clues as to the nature of his inspiration. In particular, we discern a significant and repeated emphasis on the transparent nature of the *sky* (*Himmel*). Comments Gebser:

> The predominance of the sky in the Spanish landscape, in particular in Castile, the purity, the extraordinary transparency of the light and the atmosphere, which encompasses and emphasises things, the appearance of human silhouettes before this sky, which disclose themselves differently, like nowhere else in the world, and assert themselves in a gripping manner (an assertive attitude almost like the language and style of a Cervantes); but again this sky, which rises out

---

do, however, documentation of this was not known to me at that time'; Cf. also Gebser's clarification in *The Ever-Present Origin*, 102 n 4.

of the shimmering, vibrating emptiness of the plateau: these are experiences only given to those who visit Spain.[10]

The sky of which Gebser speaks is not merely an object of external perception. It was experienced as intimately as his own body. 'The air is of such a lightness that it feels like one is breathing from the heels', he remarks, alluding to the Taoist idea that true men, primordial men, breathe from a deeper metaphysiological source than contemporary people:[11]

> When I say sky, I have the same sense of intimacy with it that our feet have with the earth. [...] Our bare foot knows much about the earth, but the knowledge of wind and star is already in our hands [...] A star is no further or nearer for us than this stone or that flower. We could pick up the stone; we could pick the flower and draw it into our presence. In the end, this also holds true for our intimate dealings with the sky. From a certain point on, what we take into ourselves is equal.[12]

In Spain, Gebser appears to have broken through to what Rilke, in the Seventh Elegy, called 'the intimate skies' (*die innigen Himmel*). The ambiance of Rilke's work cannot be overestimated

---

10 Gebser, *Rilke und Spanien*, in *Gesamtausgabe*, I, 49.
11 Cf. Zhuang Zhou VI, 2: 'The True men of old did not dream when they slept, had no anxiety when they awoke, and did not care that their food should be pleasant. Their breathing came deep and silently. The breathing of the true man comes (even) from his heels, while men generally breathe (only) from their throats'. *The Writings of Chuang Tzu*, trans. James Legge (Oxford: Oxford University Press, 1891).
12 Gebser, *Aussagen: Ein Merk- und Spiegelbuch des Hintergrundes; Notizen und Tagebuchaufzeichnungen 1922–1973*, in *Gesamtausgabe*, VII, 262.

here. Gebser was not only following Rilke's sources of inspiration in Spain, he sought and was ultimately inspired by the same *muse* as Rilke. His quest to discover this muse is first crystallised in the experience of a sky that lends the perception of reality a diaphanous character that transforms the way 'things' disclose themselves. Ultimately, however, it opened him up to that 'space' so particular to Rilke—that 'cosmic interiority' (*Weltinnenraum*) in which the veil between inner and outer melts away entirely to reveal one continuum. As Rilke wrote in 1914:

> A single expanse stretches through every being
> An interior cosmos. Birds fly in silence
> right through us.[13]

Rilke's *Weltinnenraum* is a word which condenses the term for cosmic space (*Weltraum*) with the adjective for inner, or interior (*innen*). What I have rendered here as 'interior cosmos', others have given as 'inner space', 'inner universe', or even 'inniverse'. Each rendition helps circumambulate the Rilkean reality that Gebser found and entered; a reality characterised by a vast, diaphanous fluidity between one's innermost being and the unbound expanse of reality.

These themes would also recur in Gebser's later poetic works. In his 'Winter Poem' (*Wintergedicht*, 1944), which he penned in one continuous sitting, without making a single revision or correction, and which Rudolf Hämmerli describes as the 'poetic ex-

---

13 Rilke, 'Es winkt zu Fühlung…' from *Die Gedichte 1910 bis 1922* (München oder Irschenhausen, August/September 1914): 'Durch alle Wesen reicht der eine Raum: / Weltinnenraum. Die Vögel fliegen still / durch uns hindurch'. For discussion see Rainer Maria Rilke, *Inner Sky: Poems, Notes, Dreams*, trans. Damion Searles (Jaffrey, New Hampshire: David R Godine, 2010), 177.

pression [*Fassung*] of *The Ever-Present Origin*', Gebser would write at length on the brilliant transparency intimated by the white of the winter sky.[14] Here again, the sky is as palpable as earth, stone, or flower:

> The shining winter sky
> is close enough to touch;
> and you too are this sky.
> No reason to distinguish.
> For all the stars flow through your veins.[15]

Like Rilke's 'intimate skies', the expanse of the universe is so close—so present to one's being—that any rigid division between internal and external, self and universe, is dissolved. Hence there is 'no reason to distinguish', for it is precisely this division of experience into near and far, inside and outside—in short, into subject-object duality—that prevents us from opening up into the stream of appearances and allowing its surging origins to course through our beings.

The dissolution of duality, however, also has a darker side. The celestial and the underworldly are also one continuum, and this was especially true for Gebser. In opening himself up so intimately to unveiled reality, he effectively evoked the presence of the dead. In order to understand what this means we must delve into Gebser's childhood. For it is here that we first discern the deeper roots of his personal relationship with the dead that, along with the sky, flowered most fully to his awareness in Spain.

---

14 Rudolf Hämmerli, 'Nachwort des Herausgebers', in *Gesamtausgabe*, VII, 424.
15 Gebser, 'Wintergedicht', in *Gesamtausgabe*, VII, 129.

THE EVER-PRESENCE OF THE DEAD

Her name was Ilse, and she died when Gebser was two. She was his sister, and was a year older than him. Although she departed early, her presence remained with him. A few years later, at the age of six, he disappeared one day whilst hunting for Easter eggs. Frantic, his parents found him later that evening calmly sitting at his sister's grave, speaking 'very earnestly with the dead'.[16]

Gebser recalls that while his sister was 'here' for only a short time, during that time she was never *entirely* here. Like him, she was from 'someplace else'. There was an 'otherworldliness' or 'beyondness' about her (*Unhiesigkeit*). 'This *Unhiesigkeit* I have in common with her', he remarks. 'In any event, I remained in life; but always, as it were, with only one foot'.[17]

Gebser intimates that his sister's death brought about an awareness of the ever-presence of the dead within the integral structure of life. That is to say, Ilse's death lead Gebser beyond the pervasive dualistic structures of western cosmology in which the dead and the living are fundamentally disconnected presences. Rather, for Gebser, not only do the dead always accompany us, we are intimately connected to them. Moreover, they can help or harm us just as we can help or harm them. In a touching account of his sister's death, he likens our participation in the realm of the dead to the reciprocal process of vitality and decline between the 'wine in Spring' and the 'berry-stains in autumn':

> In spring, when the heidelberry preserve is accidentally spilt on the tablecloth, the cleaning lady has to go to a lot of trou-

---
16 'Die schlafenden Jahre', 342.
17 Ibid.

ble to wash the stains out. And some always remain. In autumn, however, six months later, when the berries on the branches dry out and begin to die, the stains wash out of the cloth without any effort.

If the grape harvest was in autumn, then the grapevines begin to bloom six months later. They have a very short flourishing period, but an uncommonly fine and delicate scent. At the same time, the wine in the cellar begins to ferment and it will only settle again in the barrels and bottles when the flourishing [of the vines] has died away.

The fact that something changes its state or its form from what it once was does not mean that it has disappeared from the world; it is perhaps, as one says, dead; but you see yourself how little this actually means. For everything that hasn't been born yet or that hasn't happened yet, thus everything that one in an almost despairing way calls the future, must also be dead.[18]

This delicate understanding of death as intimately interwoven into the world of the living gave Gebser an especially profound insight into Rilke's perceptual breakthrough. Indeed, when reading *Rilke and Spain* with Gebser's own experiences in mind, one gains the distinct impression that his comments on Rilke closely reflect his own intuitions:

The division of existence into a visible part and an invisible part (the earthly world and the heavenly or divine world) creates as a consequence an existential condition in which

---

18 'Die schlafenden Jahre', 341.

both are instantly divorced from each other. [...] [Rilke] had not only passed through things, he had actually transcended that border: he stood in death. He had the impression of being in empty space, in the emptiness beyond, a situation that not only had validity for him personally, but also more generally for the entire contemporary western world, a situation that had its origin in the spiritual revolution at the end of the last century. In Rilke, however, this general situation crystallised itself in a single person: the angst that this situation evokes takes on an impersonal character from that point in time on, as I have already said. [...] Little by little he united the worlds until their borders were extinguished [...] [Here], the affirmation of life is at the same time an affirmation of death; furthermore: he stands in both realms at the same time, because he has dissolved their borders.[19]

Dissolving the walls of the dualistically separated world was, for Gebser, ultimately integral to his understanding of diaphany, for as both Rilke and Klee suggest, diaphany is not merely the ability to see 'through' things, but to see the roots of things brimming up through the surface of things. It is to see two sides at once. 'Two years ago', wrote Gebser in 1938, 'in the Summer of 1936, on the occasion of my Rilke essay, I wrote of the two sides of things, which are turned both towards and away from us, and what I meant was that, if we could succeed in getting beyond the side that is turned away from us, we would stand at once in the midst of life and in

---

19 *Rilke und Spanien*, 45–46.

the midst of death'.[20] 'With our human senses', he continues, 'we only perceive the sides of things that are turned towards us. I believe that there are faculties within us that can also experience the other side'.[21]

This motif of opening up to the other side of things, the side that is turned away from us, gains distinct expression in Gebser's 'Poem of the Dead' (*Totengedicht*, 1945), which was written the year after his *Wintergedicht*. Herein, Gebser likens our existence to a room in which the 'things of life', our basic furniture and other utilities, are already, at the same time, 'things of death'. We move in, set ourselves up, furnish our space, and although we habitually see only one side of existence, the side turned toward us, in reality we exist in the 'twin current of the great breathing'.[22] We dwell on the divide between 'life and death', 'silence and sound'.[23] And the walls of this room begin to open up:

> don't forget
> this, these walls, have yet another side:
> these things, which seem immovable to you,
> are full of transformation[24]

In this passage Gebser plays on the relationship between the word *Wand*, 'wall', and *Wandlung*, 'transformation'. There is a rich etymological background behind the poetic forms that Gebser uses to suggest a wall can bend or transform. In German, *Wand*

20 *Aussagen*, 262.
21 Ibid.
22 'Totengedicht', in *Gesamtausgabe*, VII, 143.
23 Ibid.
24 Ibid.

originally refers to walls made from wicker-work, a woven lattice; the term traces back to a thin branch of wood that bends, like wattle. This is also the basis of the English word 'wand', a stick or staff, which originally would have been flexible rather than rigid. Derived from Proto-Germanic *wend-*, 'to turn', German *Wand* is also cognate with the English verbs 'wend' and 'wind', which also have closer German equivalents in the verbs *winden*, 'to wind', and *wenden*, 'to turn'.

> And so the walls will transform
> as an inner window
> opens behind the soul;
> whether bed or grave,
> a pitcher of tears,
> or simply a fountain,
> it means the same thing:
> Deep sleep could well be high waking,
> for what gnaws,
> when bright day besets you,
> nurtures,
> when night closes in.[25]

Before we conclude, two final comments may be cited to enhance the sense of symmetry implicit in Gebser's 'great breathing'. The first pertains to Frederico García Lorca (1898–1936), the Spanish poet and dramatist who Gebser not only befriended, but closely collaborated with before he was murdered at the outbreak of the Spanish Civil War. In his memoir of Lorca, Gebser interprets the

---

25 'Totengedicht', 147.

sketches that the Spanish poet made before his death, 'which were without a doubt composed in the last nine months of his life', as expressing foreknowledge of his demise: 'the death that he felt ahead of time', that he 'drew to himself', that was 'already in him'.[26] 'For just as life is already effective in us nine months before our birth, so too is death already effective in us nine months before we die'.[27]

In such a way, we feel the fingers of Hades long before we are swept away, for the dead are integrally present by virtue of our living. When we become conscious of this, our first reaction is understandably fear. But we should not be troubled. We should be gentle in the presence of the dead, remarks Gebser; tender before 'melting time' and 'dissolving space'.[28] In his unfinished biographical writings, he says: 'When we are born we scream and cry, when we die, we should smile'.[29] And this remark more than any other grows in significance, because Gebser actually *did* die smiling. Along with a demeanour of great peace, his deathmask in Bern preserves a deeply satisfied *smile*.

EPILOGUE

Ultimately, Gebser's ease with the underworld was not something he entertained theoretically, but lived—and died—integrally. So too his openness to the Rilkean *Weltinnenraum*. Both realisations are emblematic for Gebser of the ability to transcend dualistic awareness, to render the roots of phenomena present, and to distil the ontologies of darkness and light through the vessels of diaphany.

26 Gebser, *Lorca und das Reich der Mütter*, in *Gesamtausgabe*, I, 100.
27 Ibid.
28 'Totengedicht', 143.
29 'Die schlafenden Jahre', 376.

By way of conclusion it may be remarked that the two broad aspects that we have focused on in this short study strike a clear note of resonance with core aspects of Mahayana and Platonic philosophy. On one hand, to realise one's innermost being as not merely a 'self' but a single expanse that 'stretches through all beings'—an 'intensified sky', in Rilke's words—is perhaps one of the most eloquent and evocative expressions of the *śūnyatā* concept in a western language. More precisely, it evokes the *dharmadhatu* as 'expanse of phenomena' in a way that dissolves the boundaries not only between inner and outer realities, but between all sentient beings. On the other hand, Gebser's direct openness to the ever-presence of the dead places him firmly in the tradition of philosophy as conceived in the Socratic spirit, where *philosophia* is not merely a matter of critical inquiry for its own sake, but inheres specifically in 'meditation on death' (*meletē thanatou*): of 'learning to die before you die'.[30]

In connection to both of these points, we must mention one final experience of diaphany that Gebser explicitly discusses. It occurred many years later, almost a decade after he published *The Ever-Present Origin*. And it was in India.

As part of his extensive travels through Asia in the early 1960s, Gebser visited the site of the Buddha's very first teaching. When Siddhartha Gautama set the wheel of dharma in motion at Sarnath, he taught both the causes of suffering and the path of liberation from suffering. He highlighted the samsaric condition in which life and desire are intimately bound to aversion and death, and how the path out of this predicament proceeded through 'vision, knowl-

---

30 Plato, *Phaedo*.

edge, calm, insight, and awakening'.[31]

In 1961, the Zen Master Daisetzu Teitaro Suzuki described Gebser's experience at Sarnath as Satori (awakening).[32] 'There had been no rapture to observe', remarks Gebser. 'I was not swept away into the irrational. There was no loss of consciousness of the world. Instead, there was the overcoming of the mental-rational: there was arational transparency and with it that intensity of consciousness that had integrated both the irrational and the rational in such a manner that both were respectively available, without the possibility of being overwhelmed by them, for their bearers, the vital and the psychic, submit to the spiritual':[33]

> One cannot make this transparency visible, one cannot see it, indeed one is only able to become perceptibly aware of it (in the precise sense of the word 'aware'), through effortless intensification of wakefulness. It is more than clarity or illumination, more than transfiguration or glorification, more than radiance. One could possibly speak of it as the flashing-forth or sudden shining-through of the whole. Who participates in this is more or less purified, as if melted and remoulded, liberated from the scoria of the soul, from the narrow limitations of mentation, without in the slightest manner being lost to the world through intoxication or ecstatic rapture; rather, who participates in this finds them-

---

31 *Samyutta Nikāya* 56.11.

32 'Not irrational, but arational; that's it. This experience that you had, it was not Samadhi; it was Satori'. In Gebser, *Asien lächelt anders*, in *Gesamtausgabe*, VI, 164.

33 *Asien lächelt anders*, 164. Cf. *Gesamtausgabe*, V/2, 88, 102; VI, 159, 164; II, 318; IV, 318 n 84.

selves perfectly in order, with the deepest sense of trust, and with the sacred lucidity of origin's ever-presence pulsating through them.[34]

Ultimately for Gebser, the principle of diaphany transforms 'ordinary' reality into a vehicle for an extraordinary lucidity that goes beyond the perception of fixed things. In this sense it speaks to the heart of the world's mystical traditions in which the phenomenal world opens up into a locus of revelation. 'Things' become vehicles for an inner expanse, and the liberating nature of origin becomes palpably present.

---

34 *Asien lächelt anders*, 157.

Never Paint What Cannot be Painted
Master Dōgen and the Zen of the Brush

JASON M WIRTH

> *Here, everywhere, right now*
> *is mountains, river, and earth.*
> —DŌGEN ZENJI, Shōbōgenzō, 585.

> *The mountains, rivers, and the great earth are all the*
> *ocean of buddha nature.*
> —DŌGEN ZENJI, Shōbōgenzō, 238.

PROLOGUE

¶ These two beautiful lines from the *Shōbōgenzō*,[1] the magisterial work by the great Japanese Zen Master Dōgen Eihei (1200–1253), speak directly to and from his experience of Nature. Mountains and rivers, that is, the dynamic interpenetration of form and emptiness (Jp. *kū*; Skt. *śūnyatā*), comprise the self-generation of Nature (what Dōgen, following a certain tradition, calls 'the great earth'). Mountains, with their implacable girth and presence, exhibit the

---

[1] I have generally relied on the new, two-volume edition of the *Shōbōgenzō* edited by Kazuaki Tanahashi (Boston and London: Shambhala, 2010). Henceforth S. I also use the following abbreviations to indicate the source language for technical terms and proper names: Jp. for Japanese and Skt. for Sanskrit. Except where custom prevails otherwise, I adhere to the East Asian custom of listing the family name first. Although Dōgen wrote many things beside the *Shōbōgenzō*, all of the fascicles cited in this essay can be found in this, his magnum opus.

power of form while rivers, which can take any form but which have no form to call their own, exhibit the radically pliant emptiness at the heart of form. Mountains and rivers are not found in themselves; they are not freestanding, independently existing selfsame entities. Waters express themselves as mountains and mountains, hunkered down as they are in their form, always, in their own way, still express fluidity at their heart. Hence, Dōgen proclaimed that 'mountains' walking [its discontinuous seriatim flowing] is just like human walking. Accordingly, do not doubt mountains' walking even though it does not look the same as human walking' ('Mountains and Waters Sutra', *Sansui Kyō*, S, 154). Walking is the unified interplay of emptiness and form, which makes possible the passage of one's feet. Mountains walk on their own as do all beings in the great walking of the great earth. 'If walking ends, the buddha dharma cannot reach the present [...] This is called the mountains' flow and the flowing mountains' (*Sansui Kyō*, S, 155).[2]

Moreover, the great earth is not something wholly separate from me. It is not my environment, but rather I am inseparable from the great earth and the great earth is inseparable from me. Taken together, they are dependently co-originating in the sense of *pratītyasamutpāda* (Jp. *engi*). There is no freestanding ego-self that autonomously dwells *in* Nature. 'Saying that the self returns to

2 Dōgen is also alluding here to the Chinese landscape tradition of *sansui* painting in which the artist expresses through mountains and waters the interplay between Dao and the ten thousand things. *Kare sansui* names the dry garden landscaping tradition associated with Japanese Zen in which these forces are expressed as a rock garden. For more on this, see my 'Truly Nothing: The Kyoto School and Art', *Japanese and Continental Philosophy: Conversations with the Kyoto School*, ed. Bret W Davis, Brian Schroeder, and Jason M Wirth (Bloomington: Indiana University Press, 2011), 286–304.

self is not contradicted by saying that the self is mountains, rivers, and the great earth' ('River Valley Sounds, Mountain Colors', *Keisei Sanshoku*, S, 89).

The problem of Nature, however, is also, in an ancient way and in a contemporary way, inseparable from the problem of art. This problem, as it opens up in the confluence between art and Nature, forms the theme of the present essay. Art is not a problem merely of technique. Its guiding questions are not: How do I accomplish what others do? What is the proper method? The problem of art, rather, is inseparable from the problem of the imagination, which, as mysterious as it is in its own way, is also inseparable from the problem of the great earth. *Art, as a heightened attentiveness to the great earth, is the flowing of the imagination.* In what follows, I will attempt to explicate and defend this extraordinary claim. I will do so chiefly through the work of Dōgen Zenji, although I will engage him in dialogue with Nishitani Keiji, one of the great thinkers within what has come to be called the Kyoto School. I will also suggest that some forms of this insight are not lost on painter-thinkers like Paul Klee and Wassily Kandinsky.

DONG YUAN (C. 934–C. 962), *Dongtian Mountain Hall.*

I

IN THE SHŌBŌGENZŌ fascicle 'Plum Blossoms' (*Baika*) Dōgen again turns to the poetic discourse of his late and great Chinese teacher, Rujing Tiantong (Jp. Nyojō Tendō), with whom Dōgen had studied in China and with whom he experienced his celebrated liberatory 'falling away of body and mind (*shinjin datsuraku*)'. Dōgen, himself a fine poet,[3] makes a staggering claim about Rujing's poetry and likens it in the Tanahashi edition of the *Shōbōgenzō* to what is translated as painting (畫, a kanji read variously as *ga* or *e*, a sketch, stroke, or mark, but it can also be read as suggestive of an image, as in painting, drawing, picture):

> Rujing said:
> The original face is beyond birth and death.
> Spring in plum blossoms enters into a painting.
> When you paint spring, do not paint willows, plums, peaches, or apricots—just paint spring. To paint willows, plums, peaches, or apricots is to paint willows, plums, peaches, or apricots. It is not yet painting spring.
> It is not that spring cannot be painted, but aside from Rujing, there is no one in India or China who has painted spring. He alone was a sharp-pointed brush that painted spring.
> This spring is spring in the painting as it enters into a painting. He does not use other means, but lets plum blossoms initiate spring.

---

[3] See Steven Heine's valuable book, *The Zen Poetry of Dōgen: Verses from the Mountain of Eternal Peace* (North Clarendon, Vermont: Tuttle, 1997).

He lets spring enter into a painting and into a tree.
This is skillful means (*upāya*). (S, 588–89)

Dōgen, employing hyperbole ('aside from Rujing, there is no one in India or China who has painted spring'), is insisting on something very rare about artistic images (畫): *the image is not a representation*. Painting does not reproduce the forms of Nature with either word or ink. Rujing's 畫, here in the presentation of a poetic image ('Spring in plum blossoms enters into a painting'), demanded that Rujing himself in some way become 'a sharp-pointed brush' and not just use the brush. Spring in the event of its coming to be is presented in the event of its coming to be as a poetic image. Spring's self-presentation is presented in the image. Rujing does not paint spring as an object for a painter-subject, but rather 'lets plum blossoms initiate spring.' They can only initiate spring if Rujing forgets himself as either a subject or an object and experiences himself as no longer separate from spring's self-presentation and, indeed, from Nature's ongoing self-presentation.

One could say that the self-presentation of Nature as painting can in part be expressed through the double meaning of the English word 'realization'. As Nishitani Keiji explained his phrase the 'self-awareness of reality':

> I mean both our becoming aware of reality and, at the same time, the reality realizing itself in our awareness. The English word 'realize', with its twofold meaning of 'actualize' and 'understand', is particularly well suited to what I have in mind here, although I am told that its sense of 'understand' does not necessarily connote the sense of real-

ity coming to actualization in us. Be that as it may, I am using the word to indicate that our ability to perceive reality means that reality realizes (actualizes) itself in us; that this in turn is the only way that we can realize (appropriate through understanding) the fact that reality is so realizing itself in us; and that in so doing the self-realization of reality itself takes place.[4]

Rujing realizes that the ongoing event of his self is inseparable from the self-realization of Nature and that the self-realization of Nature is inseparable from his own ongoing self-realization. He realizes (understands) that Rujing as Nature and Nature as Rujing are inseparable from reality in each moment realizing itself (becoming real and understanding itself as the ongoing self-presentation of the real). In painting the artist and the artwork express the self-realization of Nature. 'Painting spring' (*haru wo egaku*) realizes not only spring, but also self-realization as such. In such painting one expresses the self-presentation of Nature directly, rather than confusing it with one of its forms. In painting the artist lets Nature say itself anew, here and now. One can even detect a hint of this in the Latinate English word 'Nature' itself. The Latin *natura* does not merely name the totality of all natural objects, but also speaks of their 'birth' (from *natus* 'born', past participle of *nasci* 'to be born'). Using a distinction in Spinoza that Schelling in his *Naturphilosophie* held dear even as he critically transformed it, one could say that most of us study and occupy ourselves with *natura naturata* (literally, Nature natured), already born Nature, Nature

---

4 Nishitani Keiji, *Religion and Nothingness*, trans. Jan van Bragt (Berkeley: University of California Press, 1982), 5. Henceforth RN.

in its having already become what it is. It is much harder to realize *natura naturans* (literally, Nature naturing), Nature in the event of its self-presentation. Yet the presentations of Nature, Nature as it has appeared, are inseparable from the event of its appearing, from the progressive natality of Nature.⁵

To be more direct: Dōgen is claiming that Spring is not *any particular form of spring*. Although April may breed lilacs out of the dead land, as Eliot famously lamented, Spring is not lilacs; it is different from the content of any particular form that we associate with spring while at the same time having no independent standing of its own. To associate Spring with particular springtime occurrences is to mistake Spring for those occurrences. 'To paint willows, plums, peaches, or apricots is to paint willows, plums, peaches, or apricots. It is not yet painting spring'. Spring is not the idea of spring as a definition or delimitation of the event of spring. Spring is not a being, but rather an experience of time by which we understand beings in a certain manner. Spring is an event that, while expressing itself as forms, has no particular form of its own and is attached to none of its self-expressions. Were all plants to disappear, Spring itself would not disappear.

Moreover, spring is a way of understanding these forms, even form as such. 'Painting spring' (*haru wo egaku*) cannot be accomplished by representing it as any of the typical forms of spring. The fruits of 'painting spring' must rather express the dharma directly. The verb 'express' itself is an attempt to express what Dōgen calls *dōtoku*. The first of the two kanji that comprise *dōtoku* is *dō*, which

---

5 For more on Schelling's critical relationship to Spinoza, see chapters two and three of my *The Conspiracy of Life: Meditations on Schelling and his Time* (Albany: SUNY Press, 2003).

is the Japanese reading of the Chinese character for Dao (道), the great pivot at the heart of the 'ten thousand things', the 'myriad beings', that is to say, the absolute nothingness that actively expresses itself as all beings. *Dō* also has a secondary valence, namely, to say or to express, with or without words. *Toku* (得), on the other hand, is to be able or capable of doing something as well as to attain or grasp something. It is quite literally in this case the ability to speak, which we can in this respect interpret as the attainment of expressivity, which is even more fundamentally the attainment or grasp of Dao, but even more complexly, it is the ability to express Dao, to say the unsayable, to realize the soundless sound and the formless form in word and works, that is, to be able to express Dao without naming it, without snaring it in either words or works. (The Dao and the dharma can be 'expressed' by these names, but these names, or any other names, do not capture the Dao or dharma.)[6]

The problem of expression also allows us to appreciate Dōgen's final claim in this passage. When Rujing 'lets spring enter into a painting and into a tree', Dōgen calls this 'skillful means' (Skt. *upāya*; Jp. *hōben*). Art is *upāya*. In the Mahāyāna traditions, *upāya* speaks to the capacity to make something true heard in the terms and conventions of the prevailing mindset.[7] In the third chap-

---

6 Gudo Nishijima and Chodo Cross translate *dōtoku* as 'expressing the truth', 'saying what one has got,' or 'speaking attainment'. 'Dōtoku' (Expressing the Truth), *Master Dōgen's Shōbōgenzō*, book 2, trans. Gudo Nishijimi and Chodo Cross (London: Dōgen Sangha/Windbell Publications, 1996), 229–34.

7 'Very generally, *upāya* refers to the different pedagogical styles, meditation techniques, and religious practices that help people overcome attachments, and to the ways in which Buddhism is communicated to others…"skillful means" arises from the idea that wisdom is embodied in how one responds to others rather than an abstract conception of the world, and reflects an ongoing concern with the soteriological effectiveness of the Buddhist teachings'. John W Schroe-

ter of the *Lotus Sutra*, for example, the Buddha explains *upāya* to Śāriputra through a parable—itself a kind of skillful or expedient mean to express the problem of skillful or expedient means as such. Śāriputra is asked to imagine a man of great wealth whose house has caught on fire and although he knows that he can easily escape, his many sons are so absorbed in their games (attachments) that they cannot see the fire raging all around them. When the father tries to alert his sons to the problem, they are 'unalarmed and unafraid...for they do not even know what a "fire" is, or what a "house" is, or what it means to "lose" anything'.[8] What to do? The father devises an expedient but technically incorrect mean (i.e., it does not aspire to be an accurate or responsible representation). He promises them the rare toys outside the house that the sons have always desired. The sons, their hearts aflame with desire, rush from the house. The Buddha asks Śāriputra if the father is guilty of telling a lie and Śāriputra already sees that the father has put his sons on the path to realization, even though they do not yet understand it. For the Buddha, this means that the teaching of the Three Vehicles was merely expedient means 'in order to entice the beings' (LS, 64), to turn them eventually from their dull minds to a direct experience of the truth already concealed within these nonetheless expressive words. It is a saying in which saying as such comes to be heard.

In this sense, *upāya* communicates indirectly, smuggling the dharma in through the disguise of forms. Although the dharma

---

der, *Skillful Means: The Heart of Buddhist Compassion* (Honolulu: University of Hawaii Press, 2001), 3.

8 *Scripture of the Lotus Blossom of the Fine Dharma*, trans. Leon Hurvitz (New York: Columbia University Press, 1976), 59. Henceforth LS.

can only express itself as forms, it has no form of its own and hence the dharma and the Buddha are already present in *upāya*. They are not elsewhere. *Upāya* is not pointing beyond itself, but rather into itself. The dharma is present, however, when it is not confused with the words and images that express it, but rather when it is experienced directly as the living emptiness within forms. Art is *upāya* when it expresses directly the emptiness (or 'original face') of form.

The problem of the emptiness of form is not unknown in modern art. For a dramatic example, one need only look at *Der Blaue Reiter* movement in Munich in the early twentieth century. The 'original face' of form is what Wassily Kandinsky famously called the problem of the spiritual (*das Geistige*), which he considered to be the problem of art as such. In his essay 'On the Question of Form' (*Über die Formfrage*), which appeared in the group's famous *Almanac*, Kandinsky articulated the problem of form:

> Form is always temporal, i.e., relative, for it is nothing more than the means necessary today through which the present revelation makes itself heard [...] *Form is the outer expression of the inner content* [...] We should never make a god out of form. We should struggle for form only as long as it serves as *a means of expression for the inner sound*. Therefore, we should not look for salvation in one form only.[9]

Art is not the mastery of form for the sake of form and in this sense art is not the imitation of Nature if by that one means that

---

9 Wassily Kandinsky, 'On the Question of Form', *The Blaue Reiter Almanac*, ed. Wassily Kandinsky and Franz Marc, trans. Klaus Lankheit (New York: Viking, 1974), 149. Henceforth QF.

one is called to represent what Nature has first presented. One needs somehow to see through form in order to get beyond form. One somehow has to see the invisible. '*Necessity creates form.* Fish that live at great depths have no eyes' (QF, 150). To see without eyes is to see freely, not in the sense of granting one's own ego free license to do whatever it wants, but rather to participate in the sovereignty of Nature's own imagination, that is, in the freedom at the heart of the coming to be of form. This freedom is not found in myself because I, like the artwork, am a product of this freedom.

In order to produce, or even appreciate, art, one cannot stop with its form:

> In daily life we would rarely find a man who will get off the train at Regensburg when he wants to go to Berlin. In spiritual life, getting off at Regensburg is a rather common occurrence. Sometimes even the engineer does not want to go on, and all the passengers get off at Regensburg. How many who sought God stopped at a carved figure! How many who searched for art were arrested at a form that an artist had used for her own purposes, be it Giotto, Raphael, Dürer, or Van Gogh! (QF, 153)

Only in becoming the fish without eyes that somehow sees can one attune oneself to the event of presentation. '*The future* can be received only through freedom' (QF, 187). As Schelling had shown a century earlier, this freedom can already be detected in the word for the imagination, namely, *Einbildungskraft*, the power (*Kraft*) of the one coming into form (*Bildung*). The imagination is the plastic force of Nature, much in the way that Catherine Malabou has so effectively deployed the problem of plasticity.¹⁰ Its freedom is the sovereignty of coming into form.

This problem was even more acutely present in the work of Kandinsky's colleague, Paul Klee, whose famous epitaph was taken from some lines in Leopold Zahn's 1920 book, *Paul Klee: Leben, Werk, Geist*, where Zahn recounts the story of Zhuangzi who, under the force of the Dao, was at home with both the living and the dead. As evidence of Klee's attunement to the Dao, Zahn cited Klee's own self-understanding: 'I cannot be understood at all on this earth. For I live as much with the dead as with the unborn. Somewhat closer to the heart of creation than usual. But not nearly close enough'.¹¹ And what was it to be somewhat closer to the heart of creation? It was the detachment from the ego-self and its passions and the awakening to the creativity of Nature. 'Do I emanate warmth? Coolness? For there is nothing to discuss beyond all fervor. I am most pious at the greatest distance' (*Am fernsten bin ich am frömmsten*).¹² Such piety allowed Klee to be present to the self-presentation of Nature as art. 'Form shall never and nowhere be considered as a result, as the end, but as genesis, as becoming, as essence. As appearance, form is an evil and dangerous ghost' (*Form ist also nirgends und niemals als Erledigung, als Resultat, als Ende zu betrachten, sondern als Genesis, als Werden, als Wesen. Form

---

10 See, for example, *Plasticity at the Dusk of Writing*, trans. Carolyn Shread (New York: Columbia University Press, 2010).
11 Marcel Franciscono, *Paul Klee: His Work and Thought* (Chicago: University of Chicago Press, 1991), 4–5.
12 Quoted in Franciscono, 331–32. Translation of this part of the passage is my own.

als Erscheinung aber ist ein böses, gefährliches Gespenst).[13] If form does not express spiritual life, it is nothing but the haunting return of the dead.

II

DŌGEN WAS NOT advocating for the annihilation of form and the elevation of emptiness as an exclusive disjunction. The excessive concern with emptiness is the nihilistic and pernicious Zen *śūnyatā*-sickness (Jp. *kūbyō*), as if one were evacuating the concrete and making some kind of headlong descent into pure—that is, merely abstract—emptiness. Art is the non-separation of form and emptiness, not the nihilistic and reactive emptying out of all forms. Nishitani Keiji, following the great Rinzai Zen reformer Hakuin Ekaku (1686–1768), warned against this. 'The "solid frozen all sameness of the *Tathatā*", the "ice of the one dharma nature", the "ice covered absolute one or absolute identity", etc. refer to those higher attachments to self and law that lie hidden at the level beyond ordinary attachments to self and law.' Only when one breaks through this hidden source of narcissism, when the 'Great Mirror Wisdom' tears one asunder, does the 'infinite fragrance' of life emerge.[14]

The 'infinite fragrance' of life emerges in what Nishitani called the 'field of *śūnyatā*' (*kū no ba*), which is 'not that the self and things

---

13 Paul Klee, *Das bildnerische Denken* (Basel/Stuttgart: Benno Schwabe, 1956), 169.
14 Nishitani Keiji, 'The I-Thou Relation in Zen Buddhism', trans. N A Waddell, *The Buddha Eye: An Anthology of the Kyoto School* (New York: Crossroad, 1982), 58. For more on the Kyoto School and the problem of art, see my 'Truly Nothing: The Kyoto School and Art', 286–304.

are empty but that emptiness is the self and things' (RN, 138). This *ba* (場) is not some place, here or elsewhere, for there 'is literally no place to stand' (RN, 15). It is not here in the sense that it is not any object, present or otherwise. It is not elsewhere in the sense that there is no place that it is not. Looking for it elsewhere, Dōgen warned us, is like running all over the place looking for your head or traveling south in search of the North Star. For Nishitani, it is the background which is nothing in itself, but which allows form to foreground itself much as the empty sky allows form to emerge. (*Kū*, 空, can be read as either sky or emptiness.) This field is the standpoint which transforms the experience of form into something no longer fundamentally formal, no longer a representation, but rather as something more intimate, vital, and temporally dynamic. It is to see in form the soundless sound and to hear in form the formless form.[15] From the standpoint of *śūnyatā*, form does not disappear, but rather one experiences *śūnyatā* in its ongoing self-presentation as forms. It is *śūnyatā* as (*soku*) this form. The '*soku*' is a kind of pivot in which in each moment there is neither emptiness nor its opposite, form—these in themselves are nothing but unhealthy abstractions. Rather, *śūnyatā*, which in itself opposes this or any form, expresses itself right now and right here *as this form*.

In an essay, 'Emptiness and Sameness' (*Kū to Soku*), on the relationship between *śūnyatā* (*kū*) and this 'as' (*soku*), Nishitani asks us to consider looking at a beautiful *chawan* (茶碗 or tea bowl):

---

15 I am aware that I am transpositioning the visual and the auditory (hearing what one cannot see and seeing what one cannot hear). My motivation for this chiefly stems from Dōgen, as shall become apparent in the third section of this essay.

The shape is the factor that gives the tea bowl the name 'tea bowl'. It has the form of a utensil made to drink hot and cold water, with a hollow and an opening to contain other liquids [...] Our sensorial perception discerns the object in front of us as a tea bowl by its shape. In our general daily experience, the object in front of us receives the connotation of the general concept known as 'tea bowl' by its form.[16]

Indeed, the *chawan* as a particular instantiation of the general idea of a *chawan* is where we begin. We begin by recognizing *what* it is. 'At the beginning was the form…' (ES, 215). Yet the *chawan* is not merely either the idea or the image of a *chawan*; it also came to be *imagined* as a *chawan*. But what does this say about the imagination? It mediates the concept (you can imagine the form of a tea bowl) and the perception (you can recognize what you see), but it is nonetheless 'basically different from both'. If I know what a *chawan* is, that is, if I understand the idea of a *chawan*, I can also conjure up in my imagination an image of a particular *chawan*. I can see a *chawan* and recognize it by its idea. In this way the imagination can hold together idea and image, but the imagination derives neither from the practice of entertaining ideas nor from sensuously intuiting things. It does not first and foremost perceive, cognize, or re-cognize; it creates. It is the coming into being of something that we may then attempt to cognize and develop the habits by which to make it recognizable. In its coming to being, the image is not being perceived as already there, but as something newly imagined.

---

16 Nishitani Keiji, 'Emptiness and Sameness', *Modern Japanese Aesthetics: A Reader*, trans. and ed. Michele Marra (Honolulu: University of Hawaii Press, 1999), 214. Henceforth ES. Marra notes that *soku* also denotes 'namely', '=', 'that is', 'qua', 'in other words', and 'is' (ES, 179).

The imagination 'freely creates images' (ES, 216) and 'sensorial intuition and perception create a non-given figure'.

As an example, Nishitani recounts a poetic image from a Meiji-era monk by the name of Tairyū, who burned some incense during the festival commemorating the enlightenment of Śākyamuni Buddha (*Rōhatsu*), and imaginatively composed these words:

> With the pupils of my eyes blinded, I look at the universe.
> The frosty wind pierces my bones: how cold!
> Dust on the path back to my house.
> In the snow the fragrance of plum blossoms hits the tip of my nose. (ES, 216)

The imagination in its particular mode of perception neither recognizes nor represents. In order to see, it has to see in another way: 'With the pupils of my eyes blinded, I look at the universe'. Eyes that no longer see objects, either in an intellectual or sensorial mode, can see imaginatively, that is, see an image in its mode of origination. It is to 'see' as Kandinsky 'saw': 'fish that live at great depths have no eyes'. The imagination is sovereign, an 'unhindered' movement, 'the opening of the world as the "one" in the expression "one = many" or in the world as "opening"' (ES, 201). This opening is 'absolute' (ES, 201). Hence, the opening of the world is equal to 'emptiness [*kū*]', and it is 'non-adherent' (ES, 202). This last term, 'non-adherence', translates the important Zen term, *mu-ichi-mot-su*, 無一物, literally, not a single thing, owning nothing whatsoever, having nothing to cling or attach to (and hence a lack of substance in all things, not a thing that all things are). It hearkens back to the third line of the famous poem about not clinging even to the practice of polishing the mirror oneself by the Sixth Patriarch, Huineng (Jp. Enō). When Hongren, the Fifth Patriarch, sponsored a poetry contest to locate his successor, Shenxiu (Jp. Jinshū) composed a gatha likening the body and the mind (心) to two recognizable images: a bodhi tree and a mirror, respectively. They should be polished to keep the dust of the mundane world from polluting their clarity.[17] Huineng's poem cut more sharply to the heart of the matter: He denied that the body reduces to the image of a bodhi tree or the mind to a mirror. It is rather 本来無一物 (*honrai muichimotsu*): in itself and originally it is not a single thing. 'Originally there is not one thing' (ZS, 25). As such, it reduces to no image and it cannot be captured in any definition (it is not 'one').[18] Like water, it can take any form, but it has no form of its own and, originally not being one thing, not even water, no thing can hinder it. In our example, *kū* is (in the sense of *soku*) this particular *chawan*, but in itself it is originally not one thing; in itself it is nothing whatsoever, the 'original face' of the *chawan*. Like one's original face before one's parents were born, *kū* is the unimaginable ground of the imagination.

Nishitani links this both to the impermanence of things (Skt. *anitya*; Jp. *mujō*) (S, 182) and the problem of time, especially in

---

17 The four-line gatha in the original: 'The body is the tree of enlightenment [身是菩提樹], The mind is like a bright mirror's stand [心如明鏡臺]. Time after time polish it diligently [時時勤拂拭] So that no dust can collect [使惹塵埃]'. Trans. Stephen Addiss, *Zen Sourcebook: Traditional Documents from China, Korea, and Japan*, ed. Stephen Addiss, with Stanley Lombardo and Judith Roitman (Indianapolis: Hackett Publishing, 2008), 23. Henceforth ZS.
18 Huineng's gatha reads: 'Enlightenment is not a tree [菩提本無樹], The bright mirror has no stand [明鏡亦非臺]; Originally there is not one thing [本來無一物]—What place could there be for dust [何處惹塵埃]?' (ZS, 25).

Dōgen's famous fascicle 'Time-Being' (*Uji*) in which time (dharma, rivers) imagines itself ever anew as being (S, 211). 'Time itself is being' (*Uji*, S, 104); 'See each thing in this entire world as a moment of time' (*Uji*, S, 105). In Nature and in the human, the imagination is the non-duality of time and being, emptiness and form. They cannot be held apart. Time is (*soku*) being; emptiness is (*soku*) form. 'Grass being, form being, are both time' (*Uji*, S, 105). Although the theme of being-time exceeds the scope of the present essay, one can at least mark the following: time is not a being. It is emptiness, but it expresses itself as its opposite (forms of being) but in such a way that time and being are inseparable. The imagination is the discontinuous flowing of time as being. It is the Spring in spring blossoms, the Autumn in autumn leaves.

III

THE IMAGINATION—the self-presentation of Nature as 'paintings' (畫)—requires that the 'fish that live at great depths have no eyes'. Dōgen expressed this when he admonished us not just to see with our eyes: 'You should see with your ears and hear with your eyes' ('Speaking of Mind, Speaking of Essence', *Sesshin Sesshō*, S, 499). That is to say, most people rightly see with their eyes, but they have not yet learned to *hear* with their eyes. One cannot hear or see the dharma as something particular. Hearing sounds and seeing things is only to appreciate form and not to see form as itself the *upāya* of emptiness. 'Actually, hearing dharma is not limited to ear sense and ear consciousness. You hear dharma with complete power, complete mind, complete body, and complete way from before your parents were born' ('Insentient Beings Speak Dharma',

Mujō Seppō, S, 553). It is in this sense that Dōgen cites a poem by Dongshan (Jp. Tōzan):

> How splendid! How wondrous!
> Inconceivable! Insentient beings speak dharma.
> The ears never hear it
> Only the eyes do. (*Mujō Seppō*, S, 552)

Or to put it more directly, in order to see, in order to authentically open the true dharma eye, we need to pluck out Bodhidharma's eye ('All-Inclusive Study', *Henzan*, S, 611), to 'see' as Bodhidharma 'saw'. Hence, explaining his teaching that 'upholding study through a billion eons and turning it into a ball is eighty-four thousand eyeballs' (every possible way in which the dharma can imagine itself), Dōgen again turns to Old Buddha Tiantong (Rujing) of Ruiyan Monastery:

> Autumn wind clear, autumn moon bright.
> Earth, mountains, and rivers reveal an eyeball.
> I, Ruiyan, glance with this one eye and encounter you.
> Alternating the stick and the shout, I test the patch-robed monks. ('Eyeball', *Ganzei*, S, 615)

In the imagination, I see as the great earth sees. 'In this way, all illuminating study is to ask for an eyeball' (*Ganzei* S, 616). It is to open your own true dharma eye or as Dōgen cites Xuansha (Jp. Gensha): 'The entire world of the ten directions is no other than a monk's single eye' (*Mujō Seppō*, S, 556).

How then does one 'paint' with the true dharma eye? In the famous fascicle 'Buddha Nature' (*Bushō*), when discussing Nāgārjuna, Dōgen claimed that we should 'know that a true expression is not done by sound or form, and a true teaching has no particular shape' (*Busshō*, S, 245). In this context, he recounts the skillful story of Nāgārjuna's self-manifestation as the full moon shape. Countless have tried to 'paint this story' but 'they have only painted the story with the tips of their brush' (*Busshō*, S, 248). To really paint, you do not represent or mimic form, but you completely become a brush. Painting navigates the twin dangers of the fundamentalism of a preoccupation with form and the nihilism of *śūnyatā*-sickness. 'If people think that Nāgārjuna's manifestation of the full moon shape is merely a single circle, they truly see a painted rice cake (*gabyō*). It is fooling others; such laughing kills people' (*Busshō*, S, 248). When Nāgārjuna 'became' a full moon, the point was not that he became a full moon. Nāgārjuna's very body revealed itself as *upāya*, as the emptiness of and as the form of Nāgārjuna. The word medicine heals no one; the representation of the Buddha is not the emptiness of the Buddha. A painting (畫) of a rice cake is not nutritious. One cannot live on either images or concepts of food.

The image of the innutritious *gabyō* (painted rice cake) refers to a story in 'Valley Sounds, Mountain Colors' (*Keisei Sanshoku*) about the great Buddhist scholar Xiangyan (Jp. Kyōgen) who was challenged by Guishan (Jp. Isan): 'You are bright and knowledgeable. Say something about yourself before your parents were born, but don't use words learned from commentaries' (*Keisei Sanshoku*, S, 87). The point is not to represent the Buddha conceptually or artistically, but to realize oneself and the great earth as the emptiness of the Buddha. Neither scholarship nor technical painting prowess realize the living, empty ground of the dharma. And so Xiangyan studied through the night, but failed: 'Deeply ashamed, he burned the books and said, "A painting of a rice cake does not satisfy hunger"' and so in search of realization he took up the preparation of actual food by becoming the monastery cook (*tenzo*) (*Keisei Sanshoku*, S, 87). When Dōgen visited Ayuwang (to visit a different *tenzo* who taught Dōgen penetrating lessons about practice and language), he was puzzled by one of the paintings and asked the guest coordinator Chenggui (Jp. Jōkei) what it was. Chenggui responded that it was a representation of Nāgārjuna manifesting in the shape of a full moon, to which Dōgen replied: 'Truly it looks like a piece of painted rice cake' (*Busshō*, S, 249). Chenggui laughed, but he 'had no sword in his laughter and no ability to tear off the painted rice cake' (*Busshō*, S, 249). Chenggui's laughter could not penetrate the husk of form so that heaven and earth could be born anew. Dōgen consequently counseled: 'Never paint what cannot be painted. Paint straightforwardly what needs to be painted. Yet, [Nāgārjuna's] manifestation of the body in the shape of a full moon had never been painted' (*Busshō*, S, 249). It had not been painted because the artist lacked the true dharma eye of the imagination.

Yet in a later fascicle (*Gabyō*) dedicated to the problem of the painted rice cake, Dōgen seems to reverse his position. The point is not to get beyond the painting of a rice cake: 'There is no remedy for satisfying hunger other than a painted rice cake. Without painted hunger, you never become a true person' ('Painting of a Rice Cake', *Gabyō*, S, 449). Indeed, in *upāya*, 'all painted buddhas are actual buddhas' (*Gabyō*, S, 446) since we should 'know that a painted rice cake is your face after your parents were born, your face before your parents were born'. If tearing off the painted rice cake is abandoning the painting of the rice cake, indeed, abandoning Nature's ongoing non-representational self-portraiture, this is nothing but *śūnyatā*-sickness. The *gabyō* is emptiness *soku* paint such that the paint expresses form itself (your face after both you and your parents were born) as (*soku*) emptiness (your face before your parents were born). Hence, when the great Yunmen (Jp. Ummon) was asked by a monk about going beyond buddhas and surpassing ancestors (i.e., not being caught in or attached to the form of the buddhas and the ancestors), he responded, 'A sesame rice cake' (*Gabyō*, S, 447).

The Buddha was present even in the burning house whose flames we do not see because we are attached to the forms that govern our lives, but it is art, whether it is the poetic word or the painting of Spring, that teaches 'the method of breaking through' and 'the moment of leaping out' ('Document of Heritage', *Shisho*, S, 171).

EPILOGUE

In the 'Mountains and Waters Sutra' (*Sansui Kyō*) Dōgen provides an exquisite gloss on a particularly recalcitrant phrase and in so doing allows us to bring the matter of this essay together as a whole. The phrase is: 'A stone woman gives birth to a child at night'. The phrase is quite poetic in the sense that it allows the imagination somehow to imagine itself without subjecting itself to a representation. A stone woman, an image that immediately suggests barrenness but also evokes the stubborn obtrusiveness of the mountain's form, somehow gives birth. How so? Birth is a non sequitur from the formal idea of a stone woman. How then does the stone woman give birth when such an activity contradicts her form? 'Do not view mountains from the standard of human thought' (*Sansui Kyō*, S, 163). From what standard then do we view them and appreciate Nature's generativity? The stone woman gives birth to a child at *night*—in the depths of the mountain's time beyond the clarity of form. Birth—creation—is the discontinuous and therefore always innovative flowing of what Dōgen often calls the 'mysterious dharma' (*myōhō*). It is the miracle of creation, of time's spontaneous generation.[19] The time of the imagination does not move logically but rather mysteriously and miraculously in unexpected innovations. To embrace the miracle of the imagination is not only to embrace the confluence of the miracle of Nature and the miracle of art—all genuine art is natural although the desire to represent is not itself natural—it is to be in the standpoint in which the capacity to appreciate art involves the same non sequitur that the production of art requires. How else does one see the Buddha in the mountain and hear the Bodhisattva's song in the stream? How else does one approach the miracle of unrecognizable and unexpected forms?

Finally, one does not have to read or compose poetry, or take out one's paintbrushes to become a paintbrush. It is already happening when one feels the miracle of the wind on one's face, or the

---

19 With respect to the miraculous, see Dōgen's fascicle 'Miracles' (*Jinzū*), where he argues that big or major miracles have nothing to do with supernatural interventions. They are the movements of the Dharma itself. 'The miracles I am speaking of are the daily activities of buddhas, which they do not neglect to practice [...] Miracles occur throughout practice and enlightenment whenever buddhas search in the Himalayas or practice like a tree or rock' (S, 287).

gift of bumping into a friend, or contemplates the fact that one is alive. 'When you see forms or hear sounds, fully engaging body-and-mind, you intuit dharma intimately' ('Actualizing the Fundamental Point', *Genjō Kōan*, S, 30).[20] In a sense, the imagination first calls for what the Zen tradition calls the Great Death, the all changing decongestion in which the mystery and abundance and generosity of the imagination is affirmed. Gary Snyder has beautifully written of this:

> We were following a long river into the mountains.
> Finally we rounded a ridge and could see deeper in—
> the farther peaks stony and barren, a few alpine trees.
> Ko-san and I stood on a point by a cliff, over a
> rock-walled canyon. Ko said, 'Now we have come to
> where we die'. I asked him—what's up there,
> then—meaning the further mountains.
> 'That's the world after death'. I thought it looked
> just like the land we'd been traveling, and couldn't

---

20 I would also like to reflect for a minute on the comparative nature of this present essay. Comparative thinking and speaking is not the comparison of our discreet selves and discreet cultures as we speak from the trap of unchanging identities and master narratives. It is not the aligning of artworks into relations of sameness and difference. Comparative thinking is not even an affair that exclusively concerns our species—it is neither anthropocentric nor another example of speciesism (i.e., all that is of value is what is of value to the interests of our species). The comparative speaks, rather, to our being as inter-being, as interdependent, as dependently co-originating. The (always already comparative) imagination expresses a self that is already in relation to what the ordinary mind ghettoizes as wholly other selves and non-selves. The cultivation of the imagination is a kind of practice of the wild, of the co-originating out of itself of the earth's imagination, which, in turn, cannot be altogether separated from the uniqueness of my own becomings.

see why we should have to die.
Ko grabbed me and pulled me over the cliff—
both of us falling. I hit and I was dead. I saw
my body for a while, then it was gone.
Ko was there too. We were at the bottom of the gorge.
We started drifting up the canyon. 'This is the
Way to the back country'.[21]

The life of the imagination is the practice of life in the back country.

---

21 Gary Snyder, *Mountains and Rivers without End* (Washington, DC: Counterpoint, 1996), 55–56.

Beauty, Desire, and the Soul of the World

DAVID FIDELER

> *The things of the universe are not sliced off from one another with a hatchet, neither the hot from the cold nor the cold from the hot.*
> —ANAXAGORAS

THE UNDIVIDED UNIVERSE

¶ Science is the search for unity, the search for understanding the fundamental patterns of nature. The very earliest philosophers, captivated by the beauty of nature, believed that nature was orderly and that there was one fundamental principle that the entire universe originated from. This principle was thought to be self-moving and the author of its own transformations. In this way, the earliest philosophers, who were known as the *physikoi*—the 'physicists' or 'naturalists'—believed that nature has the ability to create and sustain itself.

The Greek word for nature, *physis,* is the source of our word 'physics'. But like the Latin word *natura,* it also means 'birth'. *Phuō,* the root of *physis,* means to sprout like a plant. The forms of nature are always germinating, growing, and coming into being. Because of this, the universe is alive, a continual birthing—a living event of creative unfolding.

The earliest Greek philosophers—Thales, Anaxagoras, and Anaximenes—postulated a radical unity that some later thinkers found difficult to understand. There is no difference between spirit and matter, but matter is itself a dynamic, living activity. The word *psychē* means 'life', and the characteristic energy of life is movement. Because the world is ever-moving and ever-changing, it is ensouled and alive. And since the primordial root of the physical world is eternal, self-moving, and the cause of all ordered phenomena, it was also described as being divine.[1]

There are numerous ideas of God and divinity, but western people have been influenced by the Judeo-Christian idea of a creator God who stands outside of the universe, and also by the mechanistic worldview in which matter is dead and passive, acted upon by external forces. To understand the vision of the Presocratics, however, we must leave all these ideas behind. In the Judeo-Christian image, divinity has been pictured in very anthropocentric terms, much like an engineer who draws up a plan for the universe and then sets it in motion. But for the Presocratics there was nothing *outside* of nature itself. For them the two characteristics of the divine were movement and eternal activity. Because of this, the universe itself was believed to be permeated by divinity, but not a type of divinity that stands outside of the world. The Presocratics felt no necessity to divide up the universe into a type of passive matter and an external force that acts upon it. In this way the basic idea of the

---

1 W K C Guthrie, *A History of Greek Philosophy* (Cambridge: Cambridge University Press, 1962), I, 4.

earliest scientists was remarkably modern, for contemporary physics demonstrates that matter is not a dead substance, but rather a dancing pattern of activity.

Thales, the very first philosopher, saw the entire universe as a living organism. For him the *archē*—the originating principle of the universe—was water, which then changed itself into all things through a process of self-transformation. This *archē* was alive and everlasting, capable of self-organization. Ultimately, everything is alive and animate. Thales pointed out that even the magnet possesses a soul because it is capable of attracting iron. When Thales said that 'all things are full of gods', he meant that soul, or the divine power of movement and transformation, is inherent in all things.[2]

Not only is the world alive but it is also intelligent. We see that the universe is alive because all of reality is a ceaseless flow of activity, and motion is a sign of life. Secondly, the ever-shifting universe exhibits recurring patterns of order and form—and order and form are expressions of intelligence.[3] Put another way, the deployment of order and form are strategies of organization, and anything that possesses a strategy also possesses some type of intelligence. The order of the universe is not imposed upon it by some outside source, but is a natural expression of its own inner life, intelligence, and being. In this way the vision of the Presocratics very strongly resembles the modern cosmological theories of the evolutionary, self-organizing universe.

---

2 That at least was Aristotle's interpretation in *De Anima* 1.411.a7. See Guthrie, *A History of Greek Philosophy*, I, 65.

3 For a discussion of the idea of the living universe in Greek philosophical thought, see R G Collingwood, *The Idea of Nature* (Oxford: Clarendon Press, 1945), chapter 1. See also pages 3–4.

THE DISCOVERY OF THE COSMOS: THE ORDER AND BEAUTY OF NATURE

> *The universe is a kosmos, because it is perfect and 'adorned' with infinite beauty and living beings.*
> —PYTHAGORAS

> *If nature were not beautiful,
> it would not be worth knowing.*
> —HENRI POINCARÉ

One of the most captivating aspects of the universe is its beauty. On one hand, the beauty of the world arrests us, causing us to halt in our tracks. On the other hand, it entices us, leads us onward, and calls out to us. According to one ancient writer, the very word 'beauty' (*kalon*) originates from the verb 'to call' (*kalein*).[4] Beauty can influence us powerfully because in some deep, subliminal, and nonverbal way, it reminds us of our own inner nature.

In a living cosmovision, the world is luminous and transparent. It radiates a divine beauty in which we are embedded. In the modern world, however, a great confusion has arisen about beauty. Because some people confuse beauty with personal taste, they see it as subjective, 'in the eye of the beholder', or as culture-specific, rather than seeing it as an objective quality of nature. Under the spell of materialism and the quest for efficiency, the world grows increasingly heavy and opaque. We are surrounded by the beauty of nature on every side; but when we become anesthetized to the beauty of the world, the world itself becomes exploitable—just 'a natural resource' for human consumption. If we could consistently see the

---

4 For discussion, see A H Armstrong, ed., *Classical Mediterranean Spirituality: Egyptian, Greek, Roman* (New York: Crossroad, 1986), 307.

world with unclouded vision and appreciation, we would treat it with reverence and realize that beauty reveals a deep and essential aspect of the cosmic pattern. While our human *tastes* are certainly individual and culture-specific in many ways, beauty itself is rooted in the deep structure of the world.

As often happens, by destroying or despoiling the beauty of nature in the name of economic growth, we are destroying one of our most vital links with the depths of the cosmic pattern. In terms of our evolutionary heritage, we emerged from the beautiful, organic harmonies of the world fabric, but when we no longer have direct access to the living patterns and forms of nature something of our own nature is lost or forgotten too.[5] As the biologist Gregory Bateson pointed out, the aesthetic unity of nature reveals an ultimate unifying pattern far deeper and more complete than the findings of quantitative science can describe. He also wrote that the lost sense of this aesthetic unity—the common possession of all traditional peoples—is one of the most serious failings of the modern world.[6] By entering into a deep experience of nature's beauty, we are able to experience directly the vital patterns that connect flowers, starfish, galaxies, and our own human lives with the greater tapestry of the living universe. As Goethe wrote, 'The beautiful is a manifestation of secret laws of nature, which, without its presence, would have

---

5 On the human love of nature, and need for nature, explored from a biological and evolutionary perspective, see Edward O Wilson, *Biophilia* (Cambridge, Massachusetts: Harvard University Press, 1984), and Stephen R Kellert and Edward O Wilson, eds., *The Biophilia Hypothesis* (Washington, DC: Island Press, 1993).
6 Gregory Bateson, *Mind and Nature: A Necessary Unity* (New York: E P Dutton, 1979), 18–19.

never been revealed'.[7] Ultimately, the beauty that we can perceive directly at all levels of existence and scale reveals the whole of nature to be an organically interconnected and comprehensive unity.

The Greek word *kosmos* cannot be translated into a single English word, but refers to an equal presence of order and beauty. When the Greek philosopher Pythagoras (570–496 BCE) first called the universe a *kosmos,* he did so because it is a living embodiment of nature's order, beauty, and harmony.

That the physical world embodies beauty and harmony can be demonstrated in many ways, but rational proof is only required when we have forgotten our own connection with the underlying web of life. When we can view the exquisite grandeur of a forest, mountain range, or the form of a distant galaxy with a clear and untroubled heart, the beauty and harmony of the universe becomes immediately obvious—not through argument, but through direct perception. As William Blake wrote, 'If the doors of perception were cleansed everything would appear to man as it is, infinite'.[8]

In this sense, the perception of the world's deep, intrinsic beauty and harmony was the starting point of ancient science and philosophy. In the vision of the ancient philosophers, the universe itself was seen as an embodiment of beauty, which is itself a manifestation of value. Hence, Pythagoras called the universe a *cosmos*— a 'beautiful order'—and explained that the world-structure arises from *harmony* or the 'fitting together' of different elements through

---

7 J W von Goethe, *The Maxims and Reflections of Goethe*, trans. Bailey Saunders (London: Macmillan, 1906), 171.
8 William Blake, 'The Marriage of Heaven and Hell', plate 14, in *The Complete Poetry and Prose of William Blake*, ed. David V Erdman (New York: Anchor Books, 1988), 39.

proportional relationships.⁹ We can see the patterns of harmony reflected in the structure of galaxies, trees, snowflakes, in the deeply elegant forms of living creatures, and in the proportions of the human body. In the harmonic structure of the living universe, all the individual parts fit together to make up the greater whole.

For Pythagoras there could be no separation between the realms of science and religion or fact and value. The cosmos reflects a universal order, which is a fact, but is also an embodiment of beauty, which is a manifestation of value. From this perspective, fact and value are not opposed, but two interrelated aspects of the same pattern. The cosmos is a living unity in which all things are related through kinship, harmony, proportion, and sympathy. Referring to the teachings of the Pythagoreans, Plato wrote that 'the wise men say that one community embraces heaven and earth and gods and men and friendship and order and temperance and righteousness, and for this reason they call this whole a cosmos, my friend, for it is not without order nor yet is there excess'.¹⁰ Or, in the words of another ancient writer, 'There is a certain community uniting us not only with each other and with the gods but even with the brute creation. There is in fact one breath pervading the whole cosmos like soul, and uniting us with them'.¹¹

---

9 For an in-depth discussion of the ideas of *kosmos* and *harmonia* in Pythagorean thought, see David Fideler, 'Introduction' to Kenneth Sylvan Guthrie, *The Pythagorean Sourcebook and Library* (Grand Rapids, Michigan: Phanes Press, 1987), 19–54.
10 Plato, *Gorgias* 507E. This Pythagorean-Platonic idea, I believe, is the origin of the Stoic idea of the cosmopolis discussed in chapter 4 of Fideler, *Restoring the Soul of the World: Our Living Bond with Nature's Intelligence* (Rochester, Vermont: Inner Traditions, 2015).
11 Sextus Empiricus, *Against the Professors* 9.127, quoted in Guthrie, *A History of Greek Philosophy*, I, 278.

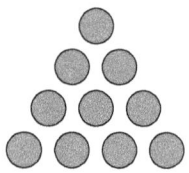

ILLUSTRATION 1.
The Pythagorean Tetractys

While the earlier Greek naturalists speculated about the structure of the universe, for Pythagoras philosophy was a broader enterprise of liberation and self-transformation. Cosmology is a search to understand the common order that embraces humanity and the larger universe. But if the order of the universe embodies a divine intelligence, that intelligence is reflected in us, too. For the Pythagoreans, philosophy and science were processes through which our essential vision of reality would become more purified and increasingly luminous. Put in religious language, by studying the divine structure of the cosmos, the philosopher would cultivate and come to know more clearly the divine element in himself.[12] By understanding our innate bond with the cosmic pattern, we also discover our essential nature.

Behind the divine harmony of the cosmos, Pythagoras discerned a mathematical order. His studies of musical harmony on the monochord, a one-stringed musical instrument, showed that the perfect intervals of music—the octave, the perfect fifth, and the perfect fourth—corresponded to simple whole number proportions. He created a symbol of this mathematical arrangement

---

12 Or, as Plato put it, 'The philosopher through association with what is divine and orderly (*kosmios*) becomes divine and orderly (*kosmios*) in so far as a man may' (*Republic* 500C).

called the Tetraktys, a pyramid of ten dots (see illustration 1). In addition to other relationships, this symbol represented the perfect harmonies in music: the octave (1:2), the perfect fifth (2:3), and the perfect fourth (3:4). As a symbol of cosmic attunement, the Pythagoreans referred to it as 'Nature's fount and root'. Where the earlier philosophers said that the essential root of nature was water, air, or fire, Pythagoras claimed that the root of nature's order lies in its mathematical harmony. In this perception, he discovered the mathematical order of nature and laid the foundation of the western scientific tradition.

Mathematics is defined today as the study of patterns in time and space. According to Pythagoras, number and proportion is a primordial, archetypal reality that structures the patterns of space and time. Through proportion, parts are related to larger wholes in the most perfect and integrated way possible. In the dynamic patterns of nature, from the unfolding of a flower to the orbital dance of a planet, there is a harmonious efficiency at work that reflects the mathematical order at the heart of creation. But for Pythagoras mathematics was not primarily a quantitative study in terms of weight, volume, or mass, but a study of the qualitative relationships and patterns that bind things together. As Einstein once said, 'The most incomprehensible thing about the universe is that it is comprehensible'.[13] Many physicists have wondered how we can account for 'the unreasonable effectiveness of mathematics', which is one of the central mysteries of western science. How and why does the universe have such perfect interconnected balance? And how,

---

13 Einstein quoted by Antonina Vallentin in *Einstein: A Biography* (London: Weidenfeld and Nicolson, 1954), 24. (Vallentin cites Einstein's 'Physics and Reality', 1936).

through science and mathematics, can we discover and understand this order in our own minds? Pythagoras claimed that like can know like. The very fact that we encapsulate the cosmic order gives us access to its innermost nature. Or as the French poet Paul Valéry put it, 'the Universe is built upon a plan the profound symmetry of which is somehow present in the inner structure of our intellect'.[14] In some mysterious way, the human mind embodies the deepest reaches of the cosmic pattern and can peer into its order.

THE RHAPSODIC INTELLECT & THE WAYS OF KNOWING

> *While intelligence treats everything mechanically, instinct proceeds, so to speak, organically. If the consciousness that slumbers in it should awake, if it were wound up into knowledge instead of being wound off into action, if we could ask and it could reply, it would give up to us the most intimate secrets of life.*
> —HENRI BERGSON

> *To know is not all, it is only half. To love is the other half.*
> —JOHN BURROUGHS

Philosophy is often thought of as a dry, abstract, intellectual pursuit. Certainly, as it developed, philosophy came to be more and more limited to the discursive, reasoning intellect. But in the beginning, when philosophy stood closer to the cosmological impulse, things were different. Philosophy began with wonder and a deep perception of the aesthetic fitness of the universe. Feeling, wonder, awe, beauty, and desire are all tied up with the innermost heart of the philosophical quest. As Emerson wrote, 'The true phi-

---

14 Quoted by Timothy Ferris, *Coming of Age in the Milky Way* (New York: William Morrow, 1988), 301.

losopher and the true poet are one, and a beauty, which is a truth, and a truth, which is a beauty, is the aim of both.'[15]

Plato was a great believer in the power of the rational intellect, but he also recognized its limitations. We need to carefully analyze problems, note inconsistencies, and draw conclusions. We need to make judgments and test the waters. But the intellect remains removed from life. It is, in some sense, artificial. As French philosopher Henri Bergson wrote, it 'treats everything mechanically'.[16] As Plato noted, the analytical intellect polarizes reality into subject and object, overlooking the essential unity that exists between the self and the world.[17] From Plato's point of view, we must develop the intellect, but we must also know how to move beyond it into a more intimate connection with the world. The intellect needs to point beyond itself to a deeper way of knowing in which there is a merging with the essential nature of reality. In this way we can enter a nonverbal mode of perception in which the sense of intellectual alienation is overcome.

In this way the intellect is limited. Like a finely crafted car, it can take us far, but at the end of the drive we need to get out, enter the living world, and travel on foot with a valued companion along the most beautiful part of our journey. As philosopher Stephen Rowe writes, 'The intellect must serve a way of being and re-

---

15 Emerson, in *The Works of Ralph Waldo Emerson* (New York; Charles C Bigelow, n.d.), IV, 40.
16 Henri Bergson, *Creative Evolution* (New York: Cosimo, 2005), 182.
17 Thus in Plato's epistemology described by the divided line of *Republic* book 6, the type of thinking or discursive analysis that rests upon a subject–object duality (*dianoia*) is a lower form of cognition than *noēsis* or direct knowledge. This central epistemological idea was later developed in considerably more detail by the Platonic philosopher Plotinus.

lating that is ultimately beyond its grasp'.[18] In order to enter the depths of the world, we need to move beyond conceptualization and embrace the vital energies that animate the universe and have brought us into being. As poet Bruce Nelson notes, the ego 'loves the hermetic, the complex and the distant—it is always stepping back, avoiding directness'.[19] Because the ego is always looking from the outside and lacks a deep connection with the inner nature of things, ego consciousness, which has strengthened since the Scientific Revolution, has assumed that the world is dead and Other. But the world itself remains alive. As Nelson writes, 'It is not a problem of a dead world, for the world has always possessed soul, but of a dead vision, one which numbs and deadens us until we extricate ourselves from it'.[20]

The word *science* means 'to know', but it comes from an Indo-European root that literally means 'to cut' or 'to split'. The same root gave birth to the word *schism*. The scientific method literally cuts reality up into little parts for the purpose of controlled experimentation. But if science and the discursive intellect are analytical, or tend to break things down, other ways of knowing are synthetic. They situate human life in a larger context. Through the knowledge conveyed by music, art, poetry, and symbolic imagery, it is possible to move beyond the path of mere analysis to experience a deeper connection with the vital energies of the world. Other human capabilities like intimacy, the unfolding rhythm of conversation, and

---

18 Stephen C Rowe, *Rediscovering the West: An Inquiry into Nothingness and Relatedness* (Albany: SUNY, 1994), 11.
19 Bruce Nelson, 'The Theology of the Invisible', *Alexandria 4: The Order and Beauty of Nature* (1997): 198.
20 Ibid., 199.

the experience of creativity all offer valid pathways that reconnect us with the fundamental structures from which we have emerged.

The beauty of the cosmos inspires ecstasy, and *ekstasis* means to go outside of oneself. Inspiration is a mysterious quality but a fundamental aspect of human experience. The greatest works of art and scientific discovery result from a collaboration between critical self-awareness and the mysterious, nonverbal depths of our inner nature. How we are able to creatively contact the intelligence of the universe remains unknown, but intuition and inspiration are as important in serious scientific work as any other factor. In antiquity, inspiration was attributed to the Muses, minor goddesses who presided over culture and the branches of learning. According to Plato, there were four types of divine madness or *mania*—not to be confused with insanity—that took the soul outside of itself to experience a larger reality.[21] Poetic madness was sent by the Muses. Mystic madness was sent by Dionysus, the god of ecstasy and liberation. Prophetic madness was sent by far-seeing Apollo. And erotic madness was sent by Aphrodite, the goddess of love. Under the spell of such rhapsodic inspiration, we are touched by an enthusiasm that carries us beyond our normal, limited boundaries.

The Presocratics, Pythagoras, Plato, and Aristotle, all spoke of the virtues of contemplation and the fact that philosophy is inspired by wonder. But with Aristotle the sense of wonder that we can tangibly *feel* in the work of the greatest early philosophers was replaced with the quest for certitude and 'verificationism'.[22] For Socrates, philosophy was not the construction of an intellectual

---

21 Plato, *Phaedrus* 265B.
22 The following discussion in this section is indebted to Rowe's work, *Rediscovering the West*.

system but a total engagement with life. He envisioned knowledge as an *event* worked out through rigorous conversation and engagement with others. For Socrates, philosophy was a way of life, a way of being, and a way of relating to the world that leads to transformation. But with Aristotle this earlier vision of philosophy came to be overshadowed by intellectualism.

For Aristotle, the intellect, rather than pointing *toward* ultimate reality in a Zen sense, became mistaken as the goal in itself. As philosopher Robert Cushman points out, Aristotle 'was subtly lured by definitive answers of supposedly enforceable demonstrations'.[23] Consequently, he 'was impatient with dialogue and preferred the declarative treatise'.[24] Writing of Aristotle's attraction to 'verificationism', philosopher Jon Moline notes that 'verificationism's paradigm of inquiry is the quest for certainty. Its methods are restricted to what are conceived to be ways of showing that a given proposition is certainly true'.[25] While such an approach is sometimes useful, its reductionism results in a greatly diminished vision of the world's richness. As the artist Cecil Collins put it, 'Logic is a superficial form of the imagination for the organization of certain local fields of activity in time and space for the needs of the creatures of humanity'.[26]

Compared with the vitality of Socrates and Plato, in Aristotle's approach contemplation lost its emotional and aesthetic engage-

---

23 Robert Earl Cushman, *Therapeia: Plato's Conception of Philosophy* (Chapel Hill: University of North Carolina Press, 1958), xvii.
24 Ibid.
25 Jon Moline, *Plato's Theory of Understanding* (Madison: University of Wisconsin Press, 1981), x.
26 Cecil Collins, *Meditations, Poems, Pages from a Sketchbook* (Ipswich: Golgonooza, 1997), 26.

ment with the living universe and pulled back into the abstractions of the intellect—a shift in orientation that powerfully influenced philosophy and theology for many hundreds of years. While we must respect Aristotle's accomplishments, as Stephen Rowe suggests, Aristotle's demand for intellectual certainty

> has led to the elevation of intellectual/cognitive knowledge over all others, and to the fragmentation and specialization of knowledge, to an 'intellectualist bias'. As a result, the greatness of our tradition, philosophy as 'the love of wisdom' (*philo-sophia*), is hardly visible as an option today.[27]

While the verifiable, deductive logic that Aristotle championed provides an excellent way to clarify an argument, the problem with all logic is that it never produces anything that is new. The conclusion is already contained in the initial premises. *By contrast, philosophy and science—as vibrant human activities—ask us to assume a greater risk by creatively and courageously questioning the initial premises of thought. They ask us to question our assumptions and look at the world in a new way.* Only then is it possible to arrive at new insights.

While all of the Greek thinkers stressed the rationality of the cosmos, the universe possesses its own rationality that cannot ultimately be reduced once and for all to simple, either/or formulas of symbolic logic. And since the universe has many faces, we may speak of it as holding a great, if not infinite, depth. From this perspective, the more sensitivities and ways of knowing we possess, the more comprehensive our knowledge of the universe will be.

---

27 Rowe, *Rediscovering the West*, 90.

Philosophy today has become a dead way of looking at the world because the world itself is complex, engaging, and multivalent; it calls out to be known in multiple ways.[28]

Yet with Aristotle's influence, philosophy began to close itself off from the numinosity of the universe and the deep experience of being by sealing itself off in the bubble of the analytical intellect. In order to revitalize our lives and our tradition, we must once again make room for art, beauty, the rhapsodic intellect, and the multiple ways of knowing. In addition to employing rigorous logic when called for, in the words of William James we need to move beyond 'vicious intellectualism' and realize that 'the immediate experience of life solves the problems which so baffle our conceptual intelligence'.[29] Ultimately, we need to go beyond our conceptual categories in order to directly experience the deep structure of the world in the most profound way possible.

---

28 For the idea that the universe possesses infinite depth and that multiple ways of knowing are required for a more complete vision of the world, see Fideler, 'Science's Missing Half: Epistemological Pluralism and the Search for an Inclusive Cosmology'.

29 William James, *A Pluralistic Universe* (Cambridge, Massachusetts: Harvard University Press, 1977), 260.

THE EROTIC PHILOSOPHER

> *The world thus exists to the soul to satisfy the desire of beauty. This element I call an ultimate end. No reason can be asked or given why the soul seeks beauty. Beauty, in its largest and profoundest sense, is one expression for the universe.* —EMERSON

By inspiring wonder, the stars and the beauty of nature excite a love for learning and exploration. Yet love is more than merely a human emotion. In the Greek tradition, the power of Eros was seen as the underlying force that moves the heavenly spheres and animates all of existence. Love is the magnetic pull that binds all of creation together into a seamless unity. When we speak of Eros today, ideas of sexual desire immediately come to mind. But our modern conception excludes the ancient understanding that sexual love is just one aspect of a much larger cosmic force. Viewed as a universal power, it is the magnetic pull of Eros that inspires the electron to desire the proton, lovers to desire conjugal union, and the soul of the mystic to desire union with the ineffable source of creation. When Dante spoke of 'the Love which moves the sun and the other stars' in the final line of *The Divine Comedy,* he was referring to the ancient idea that cosmic desire energizes the motion of the entire universe.

For Plato, true philosophy was inspired by love. When we are touched by the divine power of Eros, it sets us down a path that leads to the soul's awakening. Using a myth, Plato explained the experience of love in the following way:[30] Before birth, each human soul possesses wings and follows in the train of the gods. There, in the winged, cosmic procession, each soul glimpses beauty and true knowledge to varying degrees, feeding upon the vision like am-

---

30 This myth appears in Plato's dialogue on love, the *Phaedrus.*

brosia and nectar. Due to forgetfulness, however, the soul grows heavy; it loses its wings and sinks down toward Earth in a state of amnesia. We are all thus born in varying states of forgetfulness. When we fall in love, the vision of the beloved held in the imagination incites a form of divine madness. Eros is the desire to possess the beauty of the beloved, and in this condition 'the whole soul throbs and palpitates'.[31] The effluence of beauty moistens the hard, atrophied roots of the soul's feathers, which again begin to swell and sprout. This causes an itching and feverish sensation like the cutting of teeth. When the beloved is near, the sensation of beauty moistens the follicles of the feathers; this soothes the discomfort and fills the soul with joy. But when separated from the beloved, the follicles start to harden and close up; they prick the soul, and throb painfully like pulsating arteries.

Socrates explains that the beauty of the beloved reminds the soul of its true, winged nature. The soul is reminded of the beauty that it gazed upon in the heavenly realms before being dragged down into a state of forgetfulness. Love is a reawakening to recover our essential nature, but, in the experience of love, we often do not see what is really happening. There is a well-known tendency to fall down and worship the beloved as the ultimate source of the lover's experience, rather than seeing the beloved as a catalyst of transformation; and in the misplaced literalism of this perception, there exists the danger of not viewing the soul's awakening within a larger context. The suggestion is that an individual love, while beautiful in itself, can also awaken us to greater realities. Love is a noble end in itself, but also the means to greater ends.

---

31 Plato, *Phaedrus* 251C.

Eros leads beyond itself, but it also leads to a potentially deeper understanding of our own inner nature. For Plato, the experience of love was the beginning of the soul's awakening and education; it reminds us of what we truly are, and of our intimate connection with the beauty of the cosmos. Ultimately, there is no distinction between the beauty pursued externally and the beauty that resides within the soul. Eros demands that we go beyond our limited views of self and reality so that we can arrive at a deeper experience of our innate connection with the greater soul of the world.

In the *Symposium,* Socrates describes his initiation into the mysteries of love by Diotima, a wise and prophetic priestess. In the famous 'ladder of love' speech, Socrates relates her teachings. In the philosopher's erotic awakening, he first falls in love with a particular person. Next, he realizes that beauty is not limited to one particular form, but belongs to many. From the beauty of bodies he advances to gaze upon the beauty of the soul and the fair order of human conduct. The philosopher is next led to contemplate the beauty of knowledge and scientific understanding, and from this he is led to the ultimate vision and 'final secret', the vision of pure Beauty-in-itself. This Beauty is 'the final object of all those previous toils' and is 'ever-existent and neither comes to be nor perishes'. In coming to know the very essence of beauty (reflected in all levels of existence), 'a man finds it truly worthwhile to live'.[32] Thus the path of Eros leads from the outer vision of physical beauty toward the inner vision of expanded, contemplative insight.

In the *Symposium,* Eros himself is described as a great *daimōn,* a mediating spirit between the mortal and immortal levels of being.

---

32 Plato, *Symposium* 211D.

Love is described as the offspring of Fullness (*Poros*) and Poverty (*Peneia*), and consequently partakes of both. Love possesses a fullness and richness of being, but is simultaneously a desire for that which it lacks. The lover, painfully aware of his emptiness, desires to possess the beauty of the beloved; the philosopher, keenly aware of his lack of wisdom, desires the wisdom that eludes him. Love and philosophy are seen as an *identical* movement toward knowledge, wisdom, and the deepening of human experience. In this sense, says Diotima, even Eros is a philosopher, 'a lover of wisdom', because he too exists between wisdom and ignorance. Love and philosophy are revealed not as the idealized destinations of one's quest, but as the arduous journey itself. Philosophy is revealed as the practice of eros: the desire for the Good, or that which is best.

Psychologist James Hillman writes that 'an inflated vision of supreme beauty is a necessary idea for the soul-making opus we call our lifetime',[33] and without beauty the soul wouldn't be able to situate itself in relationship to the deeper levels of being. The world stands before us at every moment, but in order for us to really see it and grasp its nature, something in us needs to be activated. Through the power of beauty, the universe conspires to ignite our vision and passion, to awaken our essential nature. At their root, both human love and the unquenchable wonder aroused by the beauty of the cosmic pattern are part of a common erotic movement to grasp and participate in the deepest levels of reality.

---

33 James Hillman, 'Concerning the Stone: Alchemical Images of the Goal', in *Eranos Yearbook* 59 (1990): 236.

THE WORLD SOUL & THE SOUL OF THE WORLD

> *The kosmos was harmonized by proportion*
> *and brought into existence.*
> —PLATO

> *God has not made some beautiful things,*
> *but Beauty is the creator of the universe.*
> —EMERSON

According to Thomas Aquinas three things are needed for beauty—wholeness, harmony, and radiance. In the radiant forms of nature, beauty arises from the delicate relatedness that unifies the tiniest part with the greater whole, and in the natural world this type of relatedness is achieved through harmony, symmetry, and proportion. Commenting on the beauty of the physical universe, Plato called the cosmos 'a perceptible god, image of the intelligible, greatest and best, most beautiful and most perfect'.[34] He said that the universe is 'one Whole of wholes' and 'a single Living Creature which encompasses all of the living creatures that are within it'.[35]

The cosmos is a living reality woven together through dynamic patterns of relatedness, and in his famous and influential dialogue the *Timaeus,* Plato offers a Pythagorean account of how the beauty and order of the cosmos came into existence. When speaking about ultimate matters Plato would never give a literalistic description, but he offered a myth or story to point his readers in the right direction. This is especially true in the creation myth of the *Timaeus,* where he describes the underlying structure and creation of the

---

34 Plato, *Timaeus* 92C.
35 Ibid., 33A; 30D3–31A1.

universe. Plato did not pretend to offer us 'the final truth', but only a story, which he characterized as the 'most likely account'. And in this account he described the nature of the World Soul, the vital pattern of relatedness in which the life, beauty, and order of the cosmos are rooted.

The overall theme of the dialogue is simple enough. Plato invented a mythical figure, the demiurge, who brought the universe into being. *Demiourgos* simply means 'craftsperson', 'artist', or 'fabricator'. In the creation myth, the demiurge looks toward the eternal Good as its guiding light, and using this as a model, brings the physical universe into being in the extended realm of time and space. While the physical universe is not absolutely perfect because of disturbances caused by eddies in the sea of change, it is a living manifestation of divine beauty and 'the best possible image' of the Good in space and time. For this reason, the cosmos is 'greatest and best', 'most beautiful and most perfect', the physical image of the spiritual realm, 'a perceptible god'.

In overall outline the account is absolutely straightforward. The mysterious part that has puzzled commentators is Plato's description of the World Soul—the Soul of the Cosmos—that lies at the heart of the cosmic pattern. With his eyes fixed on the Good, the demiurge weaves together the cosmic soul that animates the universe. But when Plato starts describing this operation, he begins to speak of mathematics and the exact musical ratios the demiurge used to create the cosmic soul. Tuning theory, or the study of musical proportions, was closely studied by the Pythagoreans and members of Plato's Academy. As in his other dialogues, Plato included here a musical and mathematical puzzle for the contemplation of his more advanced readers.

Fortunately for the general reader, the mathematical details are not important as long as the overall idea is understood. For the Pythagoreans the musical scale was seen as the purest expression of mathematical and cosmic harmony. Through the use of simple mathematical proportions that are present in the actual universe, the musical scale is created. And through the use of these proportions, the two extremes of the musical scale or octave—low C and high C—are reconciled and brought together. *Harmonia* means 'fitting together' and *scala* means ladder. Through the perfect proportions of harmony, a continuous bridge is constructed between the two extremes of the octave. They are bound together in harmony and—like the cosmos itself—all of the parts are perfectly and beautifully interrelated in the overall pattern.

In the creation of the World Soul, the demiurge takes the principles of Sameness and Difference and weaves them together through the ratios of the musical scale (see illustration 2). Existence has two faces, Sameness and Difference, in which everything participates. In order for something to exist, it first needs to be itself through the principle of Sameness or self-identity; but it also needs to be Different from everything else. Sameness is unity, Difference is diversity. The universe is both one and many, woven out of these primordial strands. For Plato, 'The *kosmos* was harmonized by proportion and brought into existence'.[36] The World Soul is the living bond between extremes and 'partakes in harmony and reason'.[37] In Plato's descrip-

---

36 Ibid., 32C.
37 Ibid., 36E.

ILLUSTRATION 2.
Plato's Description of the World Soul

tion, *the World Soul is the intelligent and harmonious principle of proportion or relatedness that exists at the heart of the cosmic pattern and allows all things to unfold in the best possible way.*

In addition to allowing the goodness of the universe to flower forth, the World Soul accounts for the divine beauty that we can see reflected at all levels of the physical cosmos. In Plato's story, the central Pythagorean ideas of harmony, proportion, and kinship are transformed into the World Soul, the central organizing principle of the cosmic pattern. And because of the World Soul, the entire cosmos is one life, in which every part is related to the whole through proportion, harmony, and resonance.

Sameness, Difference, and Proportion are not just abstractions—they are living ideas or principles manifest in the natural world. A nautilus shell, for example, integrates Sameness and Difference through Proportion (see illustration 3). The sea creature needs to grow and change, which is a form of 'difference'. But by employing continuous geometrical proportion or 'sameness', the nautilus can accommodate change in a regular way. Through the use of proportion, the nautilus can integrate the polarities of stability and change in an ordered and beautiful way.

Many of nature's forms integrate Sameness and Difference through the use of proportional relationships. In the fractal model of a maple leaf shown in illustration 3, we can see how the part is a model of the entire leaf, and how the pattern of the whole is reflected in the parts.

Fractal geometry embodies self-similarity at different levels of scale, and harmonizes Sameness with Difference through Proportion. The pattern is the same, but it appears at different levels of magnification, as we can see in the computer-generated model of a coral shown in illustration 3. Each tendril is a model of the branch, and each branch is a model of the entire coral. Another example can be seen in the cross-section of a cauliflower shown in illustration 3. Each little floret is a model of the branch in which it resides, and each branch is a model of the entire plant.

It is the very elegance, integration, and harmony between opposing tensions that makes the cosmos an embodiment of beauty.

Nature takes the shortest route and, while exhibiting exuberant creativity, does little in vain. For as Ralph Waldo Emerson observed, 'Elegance of form in bird or beast, or in the human figure, marks some excellence of structure [...] in the construction of any fabric or organism, any real increase of fitness to its end, is an increase in beauty'.[38] As he wrote:

> Beauty rests on necessities. The line of beauty is the result of perfect economy. The cell of the bee is built at that angle which gives the most strength with the least wax; the bone or the quill of the bird give the most alar strength with the least weight [...] There is not a particle to spare in natural structures. There is a compelling reason in the uses of the plant, for every novelty of color or form.[39]

The study of harmony demonstrates why the forms of nature are so beautiful. Nature is economical and embodies its organic harmonies of sharing in the most fit, graceful, and elegant patterns. Drawing on the insights of the Pythagoreans, Plato explained that Proportion, Beauty, and Goodness are all related phenomena.[40] Good proportion—a fit relationship between the part and the whole—gives birth to beauty, and allows nature's forms to work in the most efficient way possible. This principle of relatedness is just what Plato meant by the World Soul, for the most vital principle of the cosmos harmonizes Sameness with Difference, stability with

---

38 Emerson, *The Works of Ralph Waldo Emerson*, III, 190–91.
39 Ibid., III, 193.
40 Plato discussed this connection in the Philebus, where he concluded that 'the power of the good has taken refuge in the nature of the beautiful; for measure and proportion are everywhere identified with beauty and virtue' (*Philebus* 64E).

ILLUSTRATION 3.
Fractal model of a maple leaf; fractal model of a coral; cross-section of a cauliflower.

change, and unity with diversity, and allows the beauty and goodness of life to unfold in just the right way.

As Emerson said, beauty is not arbitrary but reflects necessity. Beauty is also necessary for a flourishing life, for without beauty and elegance we depart from the cosmic pattern. Our individual souls, rooted in the cosmic soul, feed on beauty. In order to feel fulfilled as humans we need to taste and deeply savor our relation with the greater whole from which we have emerged. Nature's elegant patterns of sharing radiate beauty and goodness, a beauty and goodness that we embody in the most profound ways. When we can sense the vitally exuberant power of the World Soul and perceive its radiance shining through the forms of nature, we become tangibly aware of our innermost bond with the living universe.

Arcane Cartographies

An Interview with Timothy Ely

SABRINA DALLA VALLE & TIMOTHY C ELY

¶ I FIRST CAME ACROSS Timothy C Ely's mysterious book world in the basement of the Getty Research Institute in Los Angeles. I was sitting in the archive room of the rare book collection in my winter coat with white gloves as I lifted his craft off my cart stacked high with a combination of alchemical texts and handmade books. I opened a black clam box and in it was a limited edition copy of *Synesthesia*, made in collaboration with West Coast philosopher, ethnobotanist, and psychedelic theoretician Terence McKenna. I was immediately sucked into the pages of desert colors diluted with rainwater, and hermetic symbols that all seemed to float loosely in the makers nervous system. I was so excited by his articulation of a personalized glossolalia that seemed to engage the thickness of materials with the liveliness of his gestures, and the possibilities of magic for any who lay eyes on these pages. I, too, was inspired to symbolize sacred life in tongues. But it would

TIMOTHY C ELY, *Seer*, detail, 2014.

take an entire lifetime to catch up to Timothy—a world-renowned master of book arts fluent in the languages of metalworking, leatherworking, woodworking, and ink preparation in a way that speaks about spectrum energy, cryptography, cartography, and the possibility of internalizing time and bringing rhythm to space. His work takes an effort to experience because you have to physically journey yourself: digging into exclusive public and private collections such as the Victoria and Albert Museum or the Library of Congress to find his secret visual journeys.

ELY AT THE DRAWING BOARD, 2011.

Hello Timothy, and thank you for accepting to interview with us by answering some of our questions. You often refer to yourself as a cartographer and consider your book collections as unique forms of atlases. I'd like to explore what this means for you as an artist. What do you, as an artist, discover in your journey to create your atlases?

Once intrigued with books as carriers of information I quickly became enamored with visual reference materials—atlas books and buildings-of-things-diagram books. The first books I made were 'grounded' in maps and Atlases—and I found myself not only drawing them, but in a sense traveling on them. This was abstract tourism, being *over* a landscape rather than in or on it, and given my vivid imagination I could tell myself stories or relive my own travels through the southwest and other places—a point on a map would generate a good story. In tandem with this set of ideas came a *poiesis* from exploring words like 'crossings' and 'passage', as often the words would trigger notions for new atlases.

Can you comment on this idea that when we create we are accessing a kind of core origin?

Origins for me often invoke first principals and I rather hold to the idea that before you can walk you might become an accomplished crawler—then travel the world. Technique manifests the 'made object', and the object can be a device to focus on certain truths, so I feel that the object will serve well if made well. And the search for these core truths or trusts are not only technical and physical, but are investigations of the intuitive trails that lever up the inspiration and energy in the first place. For me there seems to be hundreds of discreet packets of events that all collude to lead me back to the core of the handmade book.

What is your attraction to ancient Egypt in particular?

For a long time symbolic, Egypt acted as a source of landscape interests because of the long horizons one finds there that are also punctuated with gorgeous geometric forms. As I began to move around the perimeter of the Egyptian motif, I kept encountering so many other reasons to keep my hands on the philosophy. The idea that mathematics, astronomy, and spiritual concepts are culturally linked and not separate disciplines was particularly attractive to me. Egypt had systems of star-watching that were astonishingly sophisticated. All this has been well covered in many other books. What is or seems unknown to most scholars is that the Egyptian mind did not view the constellations as we or other historic cultures did, and indeed they possessed not only the ones we commonly associate with the historical sky (a Babylonian inheritance), but they had an original and wholly Egyptian system of constellations. Our European constellated vision would not template over theirs. The Egyptian idea was a carefully concealed mystery source that would later add great confusion to the decoders of the Giza plateau. There is a cypher in the sky.

Do your symbols hold the same meaning throughout the corpus of your work?

The symbols I use have been remarkably consistent, and over the span of my working with them have gotten richer as I continue to gain insight. Meaning is always assigned to marks or signals or symbols, and I simply expand the notions as the need arises. Also, the idea that a symbol can project information efficiently without some of the trappings of sentence structure suggests that I can project complex arrays of ideas without using a word, and still occlude the symbol below layers of other information so that for the viewer a sensation occurs that is like detecting an unusual smell.

I sense a devotional quality to your books, almost like they are offerings to the greater universe from the base of our humble temple earth. What for you are the possible experiences to be had at the foot of an altar?

A book for me is an environment, a localized phenomenon occurring in a very intimate scale. It can be likened to a delicious potent appetizer with fantastic flavors and can only be experienced by one person at a time really (you can share but disagree on the conditions of the response). So when one is at an altar or embedded in a space demarcated as sacred, it is possible to experience transformation and it can be quite immediate. It can change mind and body quite vividly. That is what alchemy in part is about. The altar can alter.

How does this play into your understanding of alchemy?

Alchemy is a *big* deal and its very nature as occult, hidden information makes its study cumbersome. But its primary motif of *great change* is much more easily grasped. I understand alchemy to be on the physical plane, about the transformation of materials, and that this is also a poetic change. This is the change or observation felt in the heart. So we might begin with something as simple as rainwater and make note of the day it was gathered and other conditions—just that idea when combined with a pigment can make a painted passage take on a new and if not revealed, clandestine significance. There is also deep change at a psychological level that can also come from the observance or manipulation of materials with a direction towards new form.

> *You have mentioned a reference to a law of physics you once heard that the degradation of information becomes heat. How does this transmutation relate to your books?*

Often when conquests occur, libraries are destroyed. This is a famous historical idea and one that brings massive cultural alarm to those of us that love books. I see information as heat, and a good idea will make one 'hot' in an inspired, erotic, or motivated sense. This might even be why some more reserved personalities regard ideas or their generation through books or gathered groups with great or violent hostility. For me, to view information loss as heat gain takes some of the sting out of images of book burnings or physical censorship—for the information is only transformed. It is lost in the same way that a drained battery can exhibit loss but it is not gone, just moved to a very different and unavailable set of coordinates. The death of an individual is a loss of information and I take some comfort in the notion that an echo of consciousness is routine for such actions and that nothing sentient is ever really absent from the structure of reality. We are simply confounded by our inability to access it. So when my books are lost or damaged or I encounter a venerable volume that is beyond repair, I hold to the idea that the physical book object is in decay, but the information is mobile and in a sense, is in the air. The critical ideas seem never to be lost and only our limited sense of time creates an anxious sense of irredeemable closure.

TIMOTHY C ELY, *Seer*, detail, 2014.

You mention that inspiration comes from 'the objects of your longing'. What do you feel is the source of this longing and how does it relate to your vision as a cartographer of secrets?

I got lost a lot as child and sometimes feel that the longing is really a good attempt to reclaiming something that has gone missing: a book, a dream, or some unattainable goal. What is probably going on is a search for truth by using curiosity and invention and trying with some desperation, or certainly great expenditures of energy, to see what I have never seen before. This could be a part which drives authentic motivation in art and science. The grass is always greener somewhere else.

What role does uncertainty play in your research? Are you working as an artist to become sensitive to a process and terms beyond your own knowledge?

I love 'what information looks like', and it is often beautiful even when beyond comprehension. So I want to make objects that confound in some way. I love Heisenberg's uncertainty hypothesis and see many fits in other areas of life. My books should be uncertainty platforms, for if it were easy, everyone would be doing it. The destination here is a slight imbalance between the forces that motivate a visual phenomenon (the design), and the forces which motivate the creation of content and context that ultimately lead to experiencing something novel. I cannot do that if I am making a representational painting. But a diagram as imagined of a light well, or other energy field, or a geological formation can trigger unimagined connections. Then we experience a change, a shift, or a traverse to a new location.

Maps are a guide for orientation through space, what space are you guiding yourself through as the maker?

Purely the space of the mind.

In your explorations as an artist, do you see a reciprocation between depths and heights, between the ocean bottoms and the element of the heavens? Why do you think the ocean is far less explored than the stars?

The ocean is undervalued, except when it is not. This is a great and huge question and my first flash is that the ocean was once the metaphor for great distance, and in the last century the idea of the spaces between stars has supplanted that. We measure cosmic distance with time units, and the ocean with nautical miles, and they don't convert easily. I see the oceans and the stars as co-equal as operational ideas and so *as above, so below* really holds a lot of power. A small sample of seawater contains so much life, and as we learn to sample areas not on this world surface, we will find (or so the fictions of our literature predict) a richness of life.

Even though our culture is more quantifiably dominant—excelling and exalting in precision—we accept Mercator's glaring geological misrepresentation of our world, necessarily distorting the great sphere to fit onto a two-dimensional surface. How do you think this affects us?

I am taken with illusion and how we misread maps or take them for reality. Historically, our manner of finding our way in the world was to use the fossil light of stars or the horizon, and both 'things' are not there. Renaissance perspective is grounded in a horizontal line and this is the basis for the illusion of perspective. A casual study of that process reveals how it laid the groundwork for world industrialization. So a fundamental illusion, a perceptual glitch has led us to a landscape altered by mining and resource gathering and manufacturing. Here is alchemy again on a vast scale and an example of an idea transmuting world culture. It dualistically contains a dark and light side. Alfred Korzybski once said that 'the map is not the territory' and when that it thoroughly grasped, it is a winning idea. No longer will you fuse or confuse the actuality of a landscape with ink lines on a slab of matted cellulose, and if you continue to do so, it could be viewed as insane. I take art history books to be much the same—a tiny photograph of a work of art is not *the* work of art, only a bit of guidance and should not be mistaken as much more than abbreviated truth. Useful and probably harmless, but it is not a substitute for experience. So my own travels through maps carries a type of conceit for experience, for I am unlikely to travel physically over much of the world, but I have traversed it many, many times on paper: I cross vast spaces on a daily basis with the giant wall map in my studio.

How is abstraction a vehicle for the tension between truth and fiction?

All observations are abstractions in that seeing a thing is not connecting to the thing, only creating a complex of tiny histories and experiences allowing one to create that 'thing out there'. If you have not experienced something or have no knowledge of it, it is usual not to see it at all. Going slowly and carefully through the world allows me to grasp maybe more than most, but this is likely a conceit on my part, for this whole process is beyond measure.

How would we catalog all of what we see as new over the course of a day?

What truths have you discovered in science fiction?

The primary one is that science fiction has largely prevented me from being surprised. My favorite writers are like Old Testament prophets. Fiction with overtones of science seem to function beyond entertainment as a device to prepare me (and maybe all of us) to conceptually deal with the future when it shows up. The moon landing, the first cloned sheep, and unmanned drones have been delivered up to us. Sci-fi did its job so well that we can barely suppress a yawn. I know that the gloss was quickly off the moon mission project and it was terminated in part because it no longer charmed the public. I would have liked to work on that problem for NASA but they didn't ask me.

Has your interest in actual vehicles of exploration enhanced your conceptual abilities to explore the outer and inner limits?

Not too much. I think it is a side issue or something like that. It is still an area of interest, as I like things mechanical.

What books currently inspire you most as vehicles of exploration?

My atlas and the rest of the atlas collection. I have a Rand McNally from 1973, which was a gift from my father and it serves me well, though some bits are out of date as borders have moved. Then my geometry library, and book history library, and most recently a three volume set by Jan Morris on the history of the British Empire. As I view England as the top of the world and the genesis of great change, this book is verifying both the the pattern that I sense, and

TIMOTHY C ELY, *Connect the Outer Ring*, detail, 2014.

the complexity of such a viewpoint. There are thousands of books that my wife and I have gathered and all have some kind of effect.

> *You say your texts are not written to be read, but to be experienced. How does this affect what constitutes a book? Why do we record?*

So many, many things make up projectors of information, and the book form, that is the bound book as demonstrated in the forms of both the honest medieval book and the later Victorian publishers bindings are my form or canvas structures. On these forms I want to make something I have never seen, and perhaps if we are generous, we could say I am documenting my own mind. I want to know what the Universe looks like! That statement might be too outrageous, for at times I find I am working to satisfy a curiosity, or make determinate a graphic form or shape. The verisimilitude of the thing I draw sets up a kind of condition of realism, and so the diagrams look to many as real. That is a slippery thing, for reality is just a correspondence with a previous experience. A drawing will look real for someone if they have already had an experience of something, which the drawing resembles. So for me the book is made up of many formats resembling sticks or bones carrying tallies, to rolls of skin with simple alphanumeric markings, to cave walls—almost whatever device projects information and imagination. I favor a specific form of the book, but I don't reject the others as irrelevant, and certainly for specific kinds of information, like changes in the stock market, a book is inadequate. My texts or techs or *teques* (I am making this up now) are set-ups for *evoking* a response in a quiet way, and not designed to provoke or anger or prompt a position. I feel we are often at the mercy of information and we really know very little, but act as if we know so very much. A work that pushes the idea of not knowing can go some distance perhaps in softening the arrogance of a too-full mind.

> *The archetypal book is made from skins—you say your books are made from African goats. Given the texture and nomenclature*

of the book, we could even say that a book is a kind of animal or combined creature. Could you characterize what this could be?

I am more and more seeing the book as a plant with animalia overtones. Leather has been long held as both the covering material, and when prepared as vellum or parchment, the carrier of the text and image. The primary traditional adhesives are glue derived from animals and paste which is plant based. Both are useful and some traditions rely more on one than the other.

I love to look at the raw components of books under the microscope, and so to see glue or paste or a shard of vellum with inky words or sewing thread from flax is to see into the life systems of a book. Each component has a tale to tell and an idea to project. Paper especially is amazing under deep magnification, and so I see this cellular level as another poetic rub on the forebrain. The natural materials of the book seem to get more profound and more beautiful the deeper one goes.

As the codex form of the book is my medium of choice, I have also noted that the word *codex* is related to the tree and so another plant motif. It is the Latin word for 'trunk of tree' or 'block of wood'. I am fond of the original word use, and also spelling—*caudex*. The materials with which a text or image is created is also a plant and mineral mix. A couple examples: ink is often made from glue (animal) or shellac (insect) or gums (plants)—the colorant, usually black, is carbon, either from a found source, or burned from very specific materials such as pine, bone, or grape leavings after grapes have been pressed. This is only a tiny inventory and many things will yield up an ink of a preferred set of properties or even colors. Different carbon compounds or blends will give one a blue

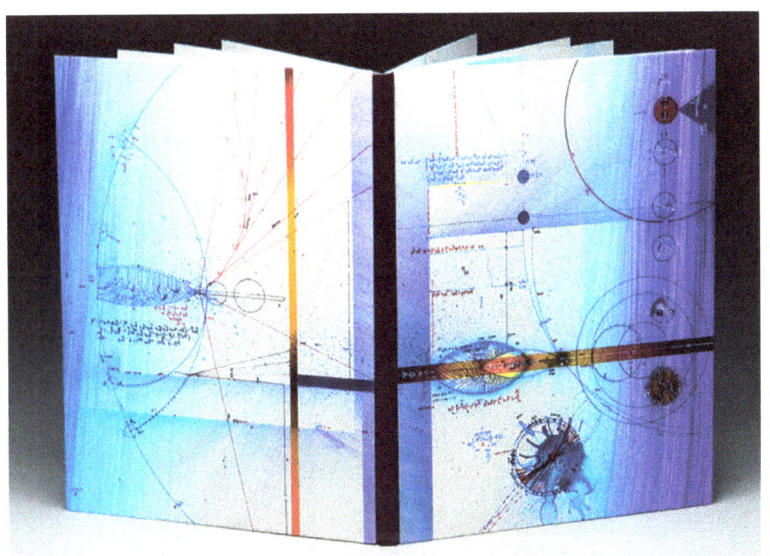

TIMOTHY C ELY, *Measure of the Hypercube*, 2004. Collection of Lilly Library.

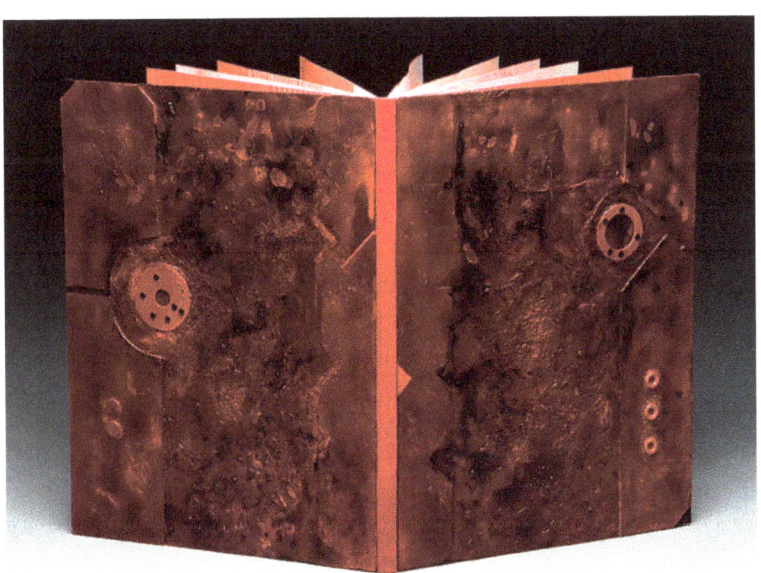

TIMOTHY C ELY, *Redshift*, 2007. Collection of Wesleyan University.

black ink, or one like the inks from our squidy cousins, a velvety dark brown. This ink in a pasta squid dish is a favorite of mine for it seems hilariously like digesting a very peculiar text.

Can you comment on this idea that the atlas of the mind's process is a function of the atlas of space?

I am guessing that they are interchangeable. Mind creates space, although the common idea is that space exists as a place to put things.

What is your favorite constellation?

I am not sure I have a favorite constellation. Once I realized, as I was working with an astronomy application some years ago, that if you view the night sky from Jupiter, it all changes. If you view the night sky from the time the caves at Lascaux were inhabited, they were different. I love that the light is 'not there' but is a fossil remnant of something that has changed position. What this means to me is that time is not real, change is real, and we use time to record or confront change. Change is the only constant. This is a fantastic notion for me. For generations we have navigated by things we hold as constants but are illusions.

I am interested in the mythology of Atlas (the bearer of heavens) as it relates to your work. Even its usage in anatomical terminology suggests a bearing of the skull as an enclosure of the heavens.

Once I used to sit by the Atlas statue at Rockefeller Center in New York and muse on the idea of a being holding the world. Overall it failed for me, for I don't see gods or God as beings, but as being—an all-interpenetrative sub-explanatory form/idea that is beyond awareness, yet penetrates awareness. (There is something in here with us in this blackend room called Universe). But I also appreciate the need to be able to discuss an experience of this being, this force, this condition of echo, and so personifying gods into divisions of labor creates for me a matrix of place or comprehension. So Atlas gets to hold my world after all and become the muse and tender for the book format. Buckminster Fuller told a teacher of mine that domes were hard for people to live in because we live inside one already—namely our skulls. The line formed by our eyes is our horizon and the sky dome of our imagination is tattooed on the inner lining of the shell. It is quite an image. So I see heaven and the heavens in my skull, in my head, and paint them from life. This is life-drawing, and the life-model is my imagination. I can work from no other.

Do we build our imagination? Is there such a thing as invisible, predetermined structures of reality?

We do build our imaginations. Many technologies exist for us to do so, from reading, to walking, to talking and exchanging ideas, to getting physical with materials and seeing what manipulating something makes us think about. I imagine that early humans thought exactly as I do, but had far fewer symbols and connections to what would trigger an imaginative epiphany.

Gradually this imaginal library gained ground and as they got the steam up, the store of images grew and humans advanced their ideas for 'what to do next'—I know that the design varieties that I have seen in the clovis spear points and other stone tools is not just an economical use of the stone but deliberate design choices. These choices come solely from an internal question, which sounds like 'what else can I do with this'. The creative individual asks this all the time, and one of my quests is to observe how often the question is asked by non-artists, people that insist they are not at all creative.

There might well be a predetermined quality to the structure of reality. I cannot get past the idea that largely due to the imaginal mind, we make up everything to make that structure fit, and will fight to the death to reinforce that idea. All of our measurements and repeatable science began with an idea, and then immediately placed whatever phenomenon was in question outside of the observational human and removed us from the equation so that reality is removed from human experience, and we then stand outside of it. I think we make it all up—all of it—and that is what makes it so cool, for the universe is us and we are it, inseparably, and we have the eyeball and organs of perception. Crude as they are, we reflect back to the universal home office an uncountable number of experiences in order for the universe to experience itself.

Can you respond to this idea that what we imagine cannot escape from what we already know? Or are there invisible structures in the living world that we haven't yet seen, that are waiting for their visualization?

I think we can only make imagery from what we know—but knowing things is a large inventory of experiences, intuition, education, and our own personal filters of what attracts and repels us. From all of that, we make new things from the stash of our lives and it can have extreme 'newness' from the impossibly high number of connections. I look at what is achieved with twenty-six letters or twelve notes in a chromatic scale, and there always seems to be new modalities in writing and music simply (sort of) by moving the bits around. It also seems miraculous when it is directed by mind, as opposed to simply scrambling letters as in a game of Boggle where most of the time nothing shows up. Monkeys and typewriters and infinity probably won't give us a Shakespeare play. But it is a distraction anyway.

I am most interested in an art that comes from deep curiosity, and one that has a touchstone that connects to many layers of culture. For me the book form as a platform for expression of these ideas is perfect, as I constantly turn to the books of the world both in nature and in the products of the hand/mind operation. There certainly are structures that are invisible—but ever-present like yeast and bacteria and a whole living biosphere that promotes and provokes us. I think there is also something like a biosphere (or some other polyhedreal shape) that is an undulating wave form of energy—electrical or static-like—which may be the carrier of some low frequency that acts as a connector for sentience. It cannot be measured at this time so it is outside of speculation and very off-topic for science. In the realm of art and of imaginative projection, it is fair game and the season is open.

$$\pi$$

Exploring the Fractal Nature of Ibn ʿArabī's Cosmology

MOSELLE N SINGH

¶ ACCORDING TO IBN ʿARABĪ, the thirteenth-century Sufi mystic, imagination is our way of accessing *barzakh*, an isthmus or meeting place for the Cosmic and the Divine. Moreover, man may embody *barzakh* as the wholly integrated microcosm of divine creation through the spiritual realization of cosmological forms. Ibn Arabī's intention is to illustrate the relationship between humankind, the Cosmos, and the Divine as a simple complexity of infinite Oneness. Yet Ibn ʿArabī and his commentators were concerned with a comprehensive cosmology, one that considered not only spiritual dimensions but also physics, astrology, and other natural sciences known to the medieval Muslim world. The comprehensiveness of Ibn ʿArabī's cosmology does not end there. An exploration of the mathematical geometrics of fractals and the most recent developments in quantum physics open up new possibilities for making Ibn ʿArabī's cosmology imaginatively and scientifically relevant.

From thirteenth century mysticism to today's scientific advances in quantum physics, we humans have used the ability to identify patterns of relations to reconcile our sense of connection in the world with our sense of separateness. Muhyi al-Din ibn al-'Arabī, the thirteenth-century Sufi mystic, presents a cosmology of simple complexity that finds Oneness in the multiplicity of forms perceived in the world. Nearly 800 years later in the 1970s, Benoit Mandelbrot uncovers the fractal geometry of nature, exhibiting a strikingly similar pattern of simple complexity. Today's recent scientific developments in quantum physics explore the unified field theory and challenge the classical separation between mental and physical phenomena. Again, simple complexity unfolds as we see that the subjective observer is not separate from the object observed; spiritual enlightenment is not separate from scientific discovery. Ibn 'Arabī's cosmology, Mandelbrot's fractals, and Einstein's unified field are all ways of understanding the same Oneness by dissolving the perception of separateness between subject and object. As we continue to attempt to understand the place from which all existent forms (including ourselves) were born, we become increasingly aware of the underlying unity that encompasses everything in the world.

Although it is not possible or accurate for me to attribute my realization of the Oneness of multiplicity to one particular instance, my process of realization was noticeably influenced and supported by these three perspectives: (1) Ibn 'Arabī's cosmology, (2) Mandelbrot's fractals in art and nature, and (3) the unified field theory. All of these perspectives illustrate an understanding of *barzakh* by

dissolving the perception of separateness through the recognition-
of the Oneness that underlies the multiplicity of forms.

THE ONENESS OF BEING

> *He who wants to know the Divine Breath,*
> *let him consider the world.*—IBN 'ARABĪ

In *Fuṣūṣ al-Ḥikam* (translated into English as *The Bezels of Wisdom*), Ibn 'Arabī explains the relationship between humankind, the Cosmos, and the Divine through the story of creation. Reality[1] first gives existence to the cosmos as an 'undifferentiated thing', operating with the innate 'disposition to receive the inexhaustible overflowing of Self-revelation', or Divine Breath, emanating from Reality.[2] This process of cosmological creation represents the manifestation of possibilities from absolute non-Being into existent cosmological forms. Cosmic Names refer to these existent cosmological forms that are manifested from the Divine Breath, the one substance of which the world is made. The Cosmos, made of the forms, is reflective, as a mirror; however it is unpolished, such that it reflects nothing of the spirit. In other words, the cosmos *receives* the Divine Breath, however, it is not able to *observe* that Divine Breath. The ability to observe is manifested in Adam, who encompasses *both* qualities of the Divine Breath and cosmological forms as the observer and as the reflective object. There are two key elements to Ibn 'Arabī's mirror analogy: the mirror and the observing subject. The mirror is that which reflects the image of the subject, while the

---

1 Reality is interchangeable with the Source, or God, in religious terms.
2 Muḥyī al-Dīn Ibn 'Arabī, *The Bezels of Wisdom*, translated by R W J Austin (Mahwah, New Jersey: Paulist Press, 1980), 50.

observing subject is he who sees the image reflected in the mirror as an object. Adam *sees* the Divine Breath and he *receives* the Divine Breath. According to Ibn 'Arabī's cosmology, the mirror is representative of the Cosmic Names (all existent cosmological forms), while the observing subject is representative of Reality, and Adam (humankind) is representative of the isthmus between the two, for he is both the mirror that reflects and the sight with which the observing subject sees. As the totality of all Cosmic Names, Adam *receives* the Divine Breath. As the totality of the Divine Names, he is the subject with the sight to *observe* the reflection as the Oneness of the Breath within himself. As Ibn 'Arabī explains, Adam is the 'spirit of the [reflected] form' and he is 'the very principle of reflection'.[3] Adam's conscious recognition of the Divine Breath within himself is the reflective medium for Divine observation.

In this analogy, Adam as the isthmus between the Divine and the Cosmos, embodies the realities of the Divine Names and the Cosmic Names. Ibn 'Arabī describes this quality of Adam as the Complete Man (*al-insān al-kāmil*), or the complete microcosm of divine creation. Humankind has the intrinsic ability to recognize the realities of the cosmological forms by realizing them within itself. In other words, by recognizing the universality of its own form in all of the expressions of existent cosmological forms, man becomes the Complete Man. As Ibn 'Arabī explains, the Complete Man is he 'who integrates in himself all Cosmic realities and their individual [manifestations]'.[4] The Complete Man does so by means of 'polishing the mirror' until the reflected image perfectly reflects

---

3 *Bezels of Wisdom*, 48.
4 Ibid., 55.

reality. When man initially recognizes the perception of otherness in the reflected image, he thereby begins polishing the mirror to achieve a more perfect self-consciousness until the perception of duality, represented by the mirror, is transcended and the mirror no longer applies. Here, Ibn 'Arabī finds 'the reflection of reality in the mirror of illusion'.[5] By heightening the awareness of the Oneness of the Divine Breath in the world, man is able to transcend the illusion of separateness between the observing subject and the observed object, and in doing so he embodies *barzakh* as the Complete Man.

Barzakh is the isthmus between non-Being and Being, between the Divine and the Cosmos, between subject and object. In other words, *barzakh* is the transcendence of dualities. It is the transcendence of the perception that the Divine and the Cosmos are separate. With this, one also recognizes *barzakh* expressed in the intermediateness of everything in the world. This recognition of *barzakh*, however, 'cannot be arrived at by the intellect by means of any rational thought process, for this kind of perception comes only by a divine disclosure from which is ascertained the origin of the forms of the Cosmos receiving the spirits'.[6] Here, imagination is the medium by which one recognizes the Oneness of the Divine Breath in the esoteric spiritual world and the exoteric corporeal world as *barzakh*, for the exoteric and esoteric are intermediate totalities of the same Oneness within the imaginal realm.[7] In other

---

5 Ibid., 48.
6 Ibid., 51.
7 Sachiko Murata and William C Chittick, *The Vision of Islam* (New York: I B Taurus, 1994), 219. Imagination is not being used in its colloquial sense that pertains to fantasy and the conjuring of unreal images within the mind. Here, imagination is the way in which man experiences his relationship to the world

words, the spiritualization of the corporeal world into the luminosity of the soul occurs by means of imagination.⁸ Ibn 'Arabī explains that imagination is the unbounded human faculty that dwells in the intermediateness of *barzakh*, such that all that it encompasses is simultaneously affirmed and denied.⁹ Only imagination is able to recognize this simultaneous affirmation and denial as One within the fabric of the Divine Breath.

The Divine Breath encompasses the infinite, inexhaustible multiplicity of forms in which it is made manifest through the process of effusion, or the act of creation. As Ibn 'Arabī explains, the Oneness of Being is 'the reality of the *barzakh*, and the self-disclosure of the Real in numerous forms. He [the Real] transmutes Himself within them from form to form, but the Entity is one'.¹⁰ The Divine Breath is One, but the Attributes (Names) are Many. While these manifestations appear in unique forms, the underlying absolute reality is not confined to the form itself, but rather it is expressed in the indefinite, transient nature of the form. This harmonious system of infinite existentiation, or effusion, of the Divine Breath from Reality reflects the continual movement the creative force itself.¹¹

'without limiting the capacity for meaningful knowledge to the restrictive operations of rational understanding' (Michael Sells, 'Ibn 'Arabī's Polished Mirror: Perspective Shift and Meaning Event', *Studia Islamica* 67 [1988]: 3).
8 William C Chittick, *Imaginal Worlds: Ibn al-'Arabī and the Problem of Religious Diversity* (New York: SUNY, 1994), 84.
9 William C Chittick, *The Self-Disclosure of God: Principles of Ibn al-'Arabī's Cosmology* (New York: SUNY, 1998), 336.
10 Chittick, *The Self-Disclosure of God*, 335.
11 Nadr Ardalan and Laleh Bakhtiar, *The Sense of Unity: The Sufi Tradition in Persian Architecture* (Chicago: University of Chicago Press, 1979), 6.

THE PATTERN OF CREATION

In everything there is everything.
—IBN ʿARABĪ

When I began studying Ibn ʿArabī, I began noticing particular patterns. I am a very visually oriented person, such that whenever I experience a cognitive process leading to some sense of understanding, I create a pattern in my mind. I connect all of the pieces visually, creating a particular cognitive design. This is how I began to recognize Ibn ʿArabī's cosmology reflected in Islamic art and architecture. These artistic representations not only reflect the Oneness described in Ibn ʿArabī's cosmology, but they also represent the creative process that permeates nature, as the two are integrally interconnected and essentially the same.

Ibn ʿArabī emphasized the importance of becoming aware of the process of creation, or *how* reality manifests in the world. The process of effusion, represented by the perpetual movement of the creative force of the Divine Breath, reveals a recognizable pattern. In chapter fifteen of *al-Futūḥāt al-Makkiyya* (translated into English as the *Meccan Illuminations*), Ibn ʿArabī explains the structure of the cosmos by its patterned nature:

> [E]ach part in every circumference matches what is below it and what is above it with its [whole] entity: no one is greater than the other, despite the fact that one is larger and one is smaller! [...] And all match the points with their entities—and that Point, despite its smallness,

matches the parts of the circumference with its [whole] essential reality.[12]

ILLUSTRATION 1. *Ibn 'Arabi's Cosmological structure*.
All illustrations hand-drawn by the author.

The Point represents Reality, while everything emanating from the Point is Divine Breath, which connects the Point with the parts of the circumference (see illustration 1). In other words, the Divine Breath (essential reality) unites the cosmic realities (circumference) with the Real (the point). Here, the self-similar pattern of 'each part' represents the principle 'matching' Oneness of Being from the 'smaller' microcosm to the 'larger' macrocosm. This Oneness is of the Divine Breath, the substance from which all cosmo-

---

12 Ibn 'Arabī, cited in Mohamed Haj Yousef, 'The Single Monad Model of the Cosmos', in *Ibn 'Arabī—Time and Cosmology* (New York: Routledge, 2008), 155–56.

logical manifestations arise. Ibn 'Arabī emphasizes that these metaphysical relations of Oneness are forever manifested to us in our observable world of existent cosmological forms. In this way, Ibn 'Arabī and his commentators were concerned with a comprehensive cosmology, one that considered not only spiritual dimensions but also physics, astrology, and other natural sciences known to the medieval Muslim world. Moreover, beyond Ibn 'Arabī's mystical Sufi writings, these patterns of existence were represented through other mediums, most recognizably in the mathematical geometric dimensions of Islamic art and architecture.

One uses imagination to contemplate the Oneness of the Divine Breath in the patterned designs in Islamic art and architecture.[13] Expressions of Oneness are articulated by means of numbers, lines, shapes, and colors to create a 'momentum-generating pattern' that bursts forth into infinite space in all directions.[14] These patterns illustrate the natural processes of creation, which form symmetrical and rhythmical patterns of order.[15] The well-known arabesque style arranges self-similar geometric forms such that the smaller forms relate to the larger whole in an infinitely repeated nature. Other styles create patterns based on the infinite divisions of the sphere, using the mathematical principle known as the Unity of the Sphere. While the recognition of the infinite patterns of multiplicity is not confined to the realm of 'Sufism', as shown here, it is also not confined to the medieval Muslim world.

---

13 Ardalan and Bakhtiar, *The Sense of Unity*, 10.
14 Ismā'īl R Fārūqī, 'Islām and Art', *Studia Islamica* 37 (1973): 100; Ardalan, *The Sense of Unity*, 9.
15 Ardalan and Bakhtiar, *The Sense of Unity*, 6.

THE NATURE OF FRACTALS

*Bottomless wonders spring from simple rules,
which are repeated without end.*

—MANDELBROT

As I became more aware of the patterns revealed to me by Ibn 'Arabī's cosmology, I began recognizing them everywhere. This is because the pattern itself is reflective of the creative process, which is what we are all observing and experiencing as we come to understand the world. The infinite patterns of multiplicity observed within the medieval Muslim world have recently been given a place and a name within western science. In the 1970s, Benoit Mandelbrot uncovered natural geometric forms of infinite complexity that spring forth from simple mathematical rules, and he called these geometric forms 'fractals'. Fractals, as Mandelbrot found, are observable everywhere in the world, from the branching of trees, the crystallizing of frost on glass, the formation of coastlines and mountain ranges, to the branching of the bronchioles within our lungs. While mathematicians had often avoided the irregular patterns of nature, Mandelbrot challenged this view and looked to nature, to that which we observe every day, in order to develop this new approach to geometry. As he found, the physical forms we observe in nature reflect more than what can be physically measured.

Fractals are difficult to define because of their infinite and irregular nature, and as Mandelbrot explains, 'I continue to believe that one would do better without a definition.'[16] Fractals take many different shapes, but most reflect the same process of scaling self-

---

16 Benoit B Mandelbrot, *The Fractal Geometry of Nature* (New York: W H Freeman and Company, 1977), 361.

similarity, known as fractal dimension. Here, the use of 'fractal' refers to the perceived irregularity of the shape, while 'scaling' refers to a certain order to the degree of irregularity that reveals itself at all scales.[17] As Mandelbrot explains, a fractal is 'a rough or fragmented geometric shape that can be split into parts, each of which is (at least approximately) a reduced-size copy of the whole'.[18] This definition of a fractal is strikingly similar to Ibn ʿArabī's description of the structure of the Cosmos: 'each part in every circumference matches what is below it and what is above it with its [whole] entity'.[19] As seen here, the recognition of scaling patterns transcends time and place.

Before Mandelbrot coined the term 'fractals', mathematicians had explored the complexity of the elusive mathematical 'monsters', like the Cantor Set, the Sierpinski Triangle, and Koch's Snowflake (see illustrations 2–3). These sets were described as monsters because of the mathematical paradox that they present. The seemingly finite forms follow patterns of repeated iteration that expose the infinite nature of their perimeters. In nature, a similar process is observed, as complex forms are born from seemingly simple sub-atomic codes.

A frequently cited example that uses Mandelbrot's fractals asks the question 'How Long is the Coast of Britain?' To begin, a straight line may be drawn from one end of the coastline to the other. Coastlines, however, are not straight—they are irregular. To get a better grasp of the actual length of the coastline, the unit of measurement used is reduced to mile-length segments in order to

17 Mandelbrot, *Fractal Geometry*, 18.
18 Ibid.
19 Ibn ʿArabī quoted in Yousef, 'Single Monad', 155–56.

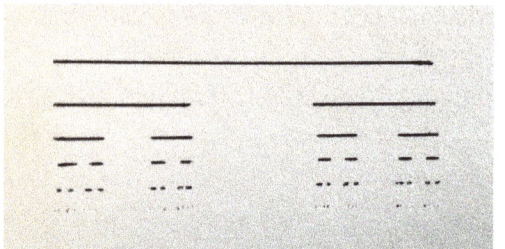
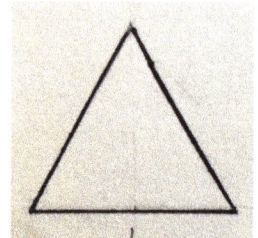

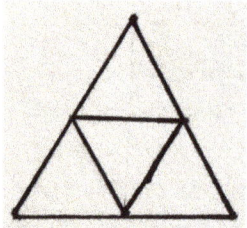

ILLUSTRATION 2. *The Cantor Set & the Spierinski Triangle. These sets were described as 'monsters' because of the mathematical paradox that they present. The seemingly finite forms follow patterns of repeated iteration that expose the infinite nature of their perimeters. In nature, a similar process is observed, as complex forms are born from seemingly simple sub-atomic codes.*

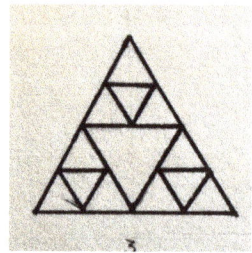

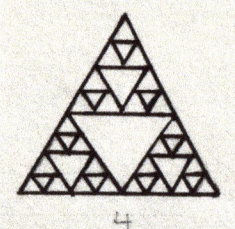

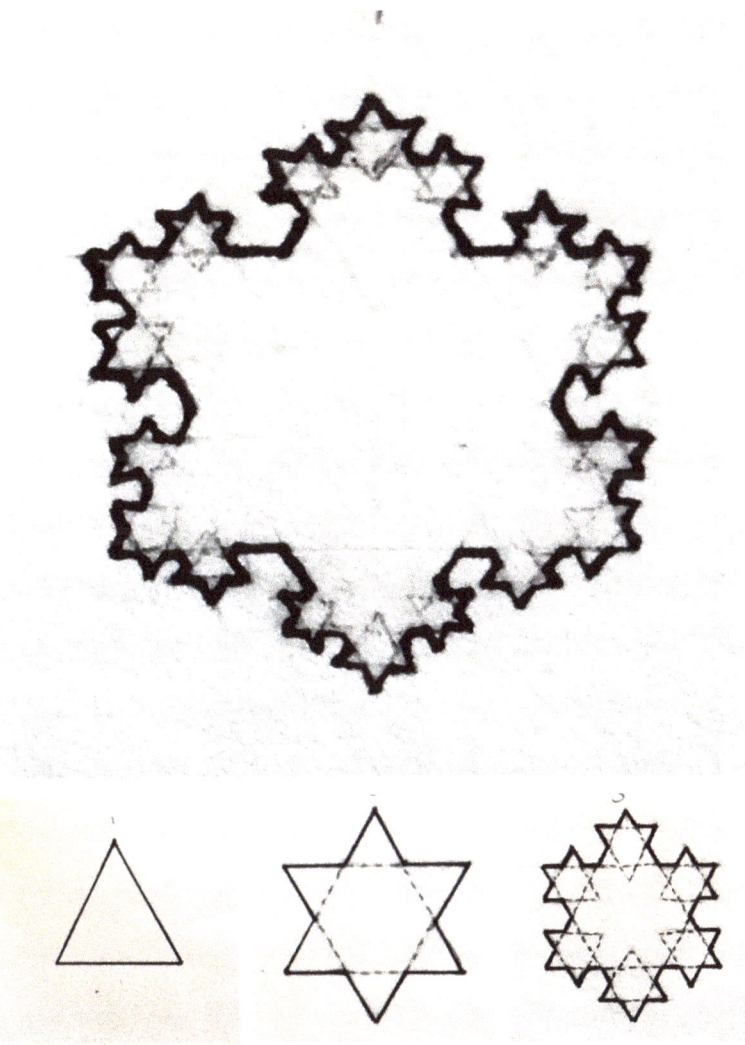

ILLUSTRATION 3. *Koch's Snowflake.*

more accurately capture the various irregularities. As smaller and smaller scales are used, however, the actual measured length of the coastline becomes longer and longer. Eventually, it becomes evident that the coastline's length is 'so ill determined that it is best considered infinite', such that as the unit of measurement decreases, the length of the coastline increases indefinitely.[20] With this realization, the concept of 'length' becomes an inadequate concept for grasping the nature of the coastline. Here, Mandelbrot proposes that the coastline is best understood using fractal curves, which encompass the perceived irregularity *and* the infinite scaling nature of the coastline.

The process of cosmological creation described by Mandelbrot's fractals and by Ibn 'Arabī's cosmology are not separate; rather, they open up new avenues for understanding the principles of the same realization. From this, fractals may be understood as illustrations of the process of effusion—as the manifestation of the Oneness of the Divine Breath into infinite iterations of existent cosmological forms, from the microcosm to the macrocosm. Inversely, Ibn 'Arabī's cosmology may be understood as a spiritual recognition of the fractal geometry of nature, revealed by infinite patterns born from simple mathematical rules, yet the two perspectives are integrally the same.

All of this brings me back to my own realization of multiplicity and Oneness. The creative pattern of effusion represented by fractals and within Ibn' Arabī's cosmology is the same pattern that I experienced through my process of understanding. I used my imagination to create (effuse) images within my mind—my

20 Mandelbrot, *Fractal Geometry*, 25.

imagination was able to translate something spiritual into observable form, and vice versa. In this way, it served as a sort of channel. My imagination was able to transcend perceived dualities to experience *barzakh* as movement and dynamism, beyond previously perceived boundaries.

THE UNIFIED FIELD OF QUANTUM PHYSICS

> *Imagination is more important than knowledge.*
> *Knowledge is limited. Imagination encircles the world.*
> —EINSTEIN

As I have discussed, Mandelbrot finds that the seemingly irregular forms observed in nature are born from simple mathematical rules of infinite iteration. These mathematical rules, however, are not where this exploration ends. Recent developments in quantum physics theorize that mathematical geometric 'strings and branes', such as fractals, are 'the source of physical objects in ordinary space', such that these mathematical principles are thought to be, quite literally, the basis of cosmological forms.[21] As these quantum theories develop, there is an increasing exploration of 'the ontological reality of geometric "objects" in mathematical, conceptual, or imaginary space and time'.[22] Here, Mandelbrot's exploration of fractals and the recent exploration of quantum physics both reflect the very real implications of the geometrical patterns that are born from simple mathematical rules.

---

21 Richard W Boyer, 'Making Room for Mental Space', *NeuroQuantology* 7.3 (2009): 467.
22 Ibid.

While I have addressed how Ibn 'Arabī's corporeal realm of existent cosmological forms reflects modern scientific epistemology, I have not yet addressed how Ibn 'Arabī's spiritual realm of the Divine Breath relates. Thus far, I have described the core aspects of Ibn Arabī's cosmology, the patterned structure of his cosmology, and the relationship of the cosmological structure to the fractal geometry of nature. At the most basic level, we may observe the mathematical principles of highly diverse geometric patterns, but an important question remains: From where do these mathematical principles spring forth? Here, we turn to quantum physics. Fractal geometry relates to the observed patterned structure of the quantum field (or Cosmos in Ibn 'Arabī's terms), but beyond this field, we may explore the unified field (or Divine Breath in Ibn 'Arabī's terms).

As the most notable and fundamental theory emerging in modern science, the unified field theory has become the core theory of quantum physics.[23] The 'unified field', originally coined by Albert Einstein, may be described as the perfect state of equilibrium, or zero-phase, that is a priori to the quantum field. It is from this field of immeasurable, infinite density that everything is born.[24] Here the 'unified field' is noticeably similar to the 'Divine Breath' of Ibn 'Arabī's cosmology. The unified field, similar to the Divine Breath, is '[t]he ultimate wholeness, or completely unified field prior to any parts, [which] can be likened to mathematical concepts of empty set, or zero, or one (Oneness)'.[25] Further, both the unified field

---

23 Ibid., 461.
24 Richard Buckminster Fuller, *Synergetics: Explorations in the Geometry of Thinking* (New York: Macmillan, 1975).
25 Boyer, 'Mental Space', 479.

and the Divine Breath are understood as constant fields of energy-substances that 'contain all potential, all order, all phenomena', and from which all existent forms are manifested.[26] With this, all of the 'phenomenal realities' observed in the world are only 'partial reflections of the total reality of the unified field, the ultimate infinite eternal'.[27] (See illustration 4).

The unified field theory also addresses the role of the observer and the observed similarly to Ibn ʿArabī's analogy of the mirror. The unified field theory logically necessitates the bridging of the gap between the observer and the observed and between objectivity and subjectivity.[28] According to the unified field theory, the conscious observer of the object creates what is observed.[29] Similarly, in Ibn ʿArabī's mirror analogy, the observer plays the key role as both the mirror that reflects the 'object' and the sight with which the observing subject sees. Further, through the mirror analogy, Ibn ʿArabī explains the eventual transcendence of the perception of duality between the observed object and the observing subject, at which point the mirror no longer applies. In both the unified field theory and Ibn ʿArabī's cosmology, the perceived separation between the subject and object is transcended through the process of increasingly conscious observation, known to Ibn ʿArabī as the polishing of the mirror.

26 Ibid.
27 Ibid., 479.
28 Ibid., 461.
29 Ibid.

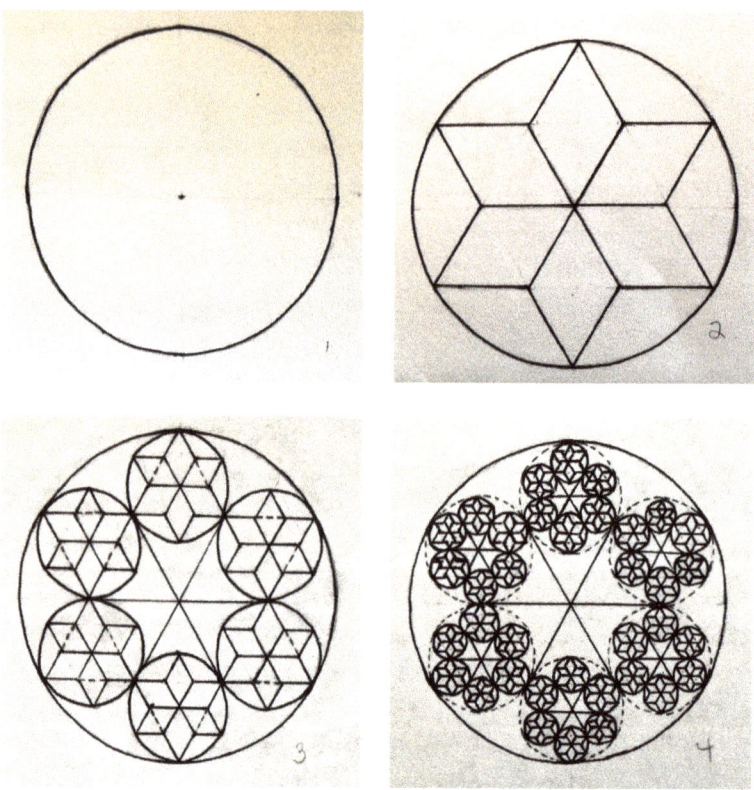

ILLUSTRATION 4. *Emerging from a blank field—the Divine Breath or unified field, from which all else is born—this pattern continues on indefinitely. The complexity and forms that can be created are infinite and indefinite. This is only one representation of infinite possibilities. Note: the dashed lines seen in 3 and 4 represent the shapes seen in the step prior.*

From Ibn 'Arabī to fractals to the unified field, infiniteness and interconnectedness are increasingly recognized as the observer uses finer and finer measurements to observe. Ibn 'Arabī emphasizes the importance of integrating all cosmological forms into the spiritual soul by conscious, self-engaged observation, and as more connections are formed (as the mirror is polished), the closer one moves towards understanding the infinite Oneness of cosmological existents. In other words, the polishing of the mirror and the awareness of measurement may be understood as the unfolding of that which is enfolded within manifested forms:

> in the implicate order the totality of existence is enfolded within each region of space (and time). So, whatever part, element, or aspect we may abstract in thought, this still enfolds the whole and is therefore intrinsically related to the totality from which it has been abstracted. Thus, wholeness permeates all that is being discussed, from the very outset.[30]

In the case of the fractal geometry of nature, as one attempts to measure the coast of Britain, the length becomes indefinite as the measurement becomes increasingly precise. Further, in quantum physics, as time and distance scales are explored, the distinction between objectivity and subjectivity is increasingly irrelevant.[31] In other words, in all of these examples, the closer we look, the closer physical and spiritual phenomena are recognized as intimately interconnected and integrally one and the same.

---

30 David Bohm, *Wholeness and the Implicate Order* (New York: Routledge, 1980), 218.
31 Boyer, 'Mental Space', 461.

While Ibn ʿArabī emphasizes that imagination, as opposed to rationality, is our way for transcending dualities and moving towards the recognition of the Divine Breath within all cosmological forms, the unified field theory also finds that there is a universal flux, or plenum, that can only be known implicitly within the explicitly definable forms and shapes that are born from the unified field.[32] Further, just as Ibn ʿArabī explains the exoteric corporeal and esoteric spiritual realms as two aspects of One totality, the unified field theory finds that mind and matter are not separate; rather, they are 'different aspects of one whole and unbroken movement'.[33] With this, just as nothing exists independently of the Divine Breath, no part of nature would exist outside of the unified field, because the unified field is 'the eternal infinite that includes everything'.[34] Here, imagination is once again attributed as the medium by which to 'get a sense of these proposed ultimate dynamics of nature involving both point value of nothing and infinite value of everything simultaneously'.[35] With this, it becomes clear that the relevance of Ibn ʿArabī's cosmology has not dissipated with time; in fact, as I have shown, his understanding of the cosmological structure of the world is uncannily similar to Mandelbrot's mathematical geometry of fractals. Further, his understanding of spiritual realities born from the Divine Breath is strikingly similar to the unified field theory of quantum physics.

This phenomenon we call life is born from a delicate balance of interconnections, from those that exist within the body, among or-

---

32 Bohm, *Wholeness*, 235.
33 Ibid., 14.
34 Boyer, 'Mental Space', 480.
35 Ibid.

gans, cells, and neurons, to those that exist among people, animals, plants, air, and atoms. In my own experience, this pattern of interconnection is illuminated by art and nature. My awareness of this pattern was dormant until I began allowing myself to recognize the presence of the pattern in everything I was experiencing. After all, I cannot separate myself from the process. I cannot rationalize my observation and that which is observed as separate from myself. I have come to recognize *barzakh* through the spiritual realization of the cosmological forms that I observe as myself.

Through my chain of realization, I began recognizing the very real presence of the multiplicity and Oneness in my own experiences. I began to sense *barzakh* as the Oneness manifested itself through forms in my artwork—through highly symmetrical and repeated patterns of fractal nature. For me, drawing is an exercise in allowing my imagination to reveal itself through creative expression. It is an active realization of the movement that reveals the totality of subject and object. Drawing fosters a sense of awe that pulls my perception outside of what I usually consider to be my physical form and connects it to another sense of existence that is interconnected and boundless. It is an exercise in letting go and allowing myself to be taken by the process of creation. To draw, I must allow myself to be vulnerable and to be moved by that which inspires—something indescribable. It is then, when I let myself go, that I experience the translation and integration of the unobservable and the observable, the abstract and the concrete, the subject and the object. This is when the observable form on paper reflects the creative process itself.

Without using measuring tools, rulers, or compasses, I am able to create these patterns. The patterns are integrally part of me and I am integrally part of them. Upon a blank sheet of paper, through an implicit imaginative and creative force, shapes and designs of definable form are born. The forms that are considered 'scientific', 'mathematical', 'quantifiable', and 'measurable' are created by an implicit, creative force that cannot be measured. This is because both are integrally *the same*: this is *barzakh*—the intermediateness of all.

CONCLUSION

Regardless of how you come to understand the infinite nature of these patterns of Oneness, the reality is that the patterns are ever-present all around us in the world. Truly understanding the simple complexity of infiniteness does not come immediately, nor does it stay constant, rather it is something that reveals itself by reflection and connection. As Mandelbrot explains, 'The nature of fractals is meant to be gradually discovered by the reader, not revealed in a flash by the author'.[36] There is not one way to discover the nature of reality, because it is enfolded within every one thing and every one thing is integrally connected as One with every other one thing. With this, there is not any one point at which the nature of reality is fully revealed because it is constantly being revealed at *every* point. One may become increasingly aware of how the points interrelate, move, and change together. This process of fine-tuning and harmonizing, or 'polishing the mirror', is done through the esoteric spiritualization of the exoteric corporeal world of cosmological forms. As Ibn 'Arabī further explains:

36 Mandelbrot, *Fractal Geometry*, 5.

Reality has described Himself as being the Outer and the Inner [Manifest and Unmanifest]. He brought the Cosmos into being as constituting an unseen realm and sensory realm, so that we might perceive the Inner through our unseen and the outer through our sensory aspect.[37]

By integrating the Outer and Inner through the increasing recognition of the multiplicity of all Cosmic realities within oneself, unified in the Divine Breath, one may become closer to Reality.[38] This is known as the polishing of the mirror—achieving an increased clarity of the integral Oneness of subject and object. We are just as much a part of this infiniteness as everything else, and realizing that relation is essential to recognizing infinite Oneness.

In the end, this paper on its own is functioning through rationality, and it is up to you to engage with your imagination to create your own images. In order for you to feel the reality of these principles, you must experience it *yourself*, in the world, everywhere in flux around you and within you—in the grooves of your own hand to the branching of the trees. Just as there are infinite cosmological forms, there are infinite processes of realization. Exploring the connection among Ibn 'Arabī's cosmology, fractal patterns, and quantum physics represents one of my most recognizable processes of increasing awareness, although the process itself is a continual, constantly changing experience of living. I have come to a greater sense that there is no separation of 'science' and 'spirituality' or of 'esoteric' or 'exoteric' observation. This cognitive process of understanding reflects the same simple complexity as that of fractals,

---

37 Ibn 'Arabī, *Bezels of Wisdom*, 55.
38 Ibid.

quantum physics, and Ibn 'Arabī's cosmology as we unite Manyness with Oneness. We are all of this One universe, so why wouldn't our cognitive processes show similar creative patterns to the growth of a tree, to the unfurling of leaves, to the development of an embryo in a womb? From Ibn 'Arabī's cosmology to Mandelbrot's fractals to today's scientific explorations in quantum physics, we may become more aware of these explorations as different modes for observing the same pattern: the simple complexity of infinite Oneness.

Never Born, Never Die

Individuation, Mutation, and Mystical Birth via Gebser's Ever-Present Origin

NICOLA MASCIANDARO

¶ THIS ESSAY REFLECTS upon the spiritual nature and significance of birth in the context of Jean Gebser's *Ever-Present Origin*. In doing so, it offers both an interpretation of the book's general elision of the question of birth and an elaboration of the traditional doctrine of spiritual birth, as communicated in the writings of Meister Eckhart and Meher Baba, two great exponents of the mystical principle that the purpose of life is that the individual realize its divinity or eternal nature in the present, now, in the midst of time. By bringing the idea of mystical birth to bear upon Gebser's account of the advent of the integrally-structured aperspectival world, a double insight is produced with regard to the imperative of birth, namely: (1) that birth is properly the opportunity to have never been born, and (2) that the way to 'effect integrality' lies not in affirming the event of birth but in abandoning hope in the identity it seemingly produces, the *you* who never was and is already dead. The argument is developed in six parts. In the first, I describe the aperspectival magnitude of the problem of birth, so as to establish that its solution must be on the order of the death of birth. In the second, I interpret Gebser's elision of the problem of birth, not as an oversight or blindspot of his thought, but as a form of spontaneous surrender or renunciation of a problem that cannot otherwise be overcome. In the third, I explore further what it means spiritually to surrender birth in light of the mystery of individuation, showing how this surrender flows from the spontaneous essence of birth itself, so that birth is surrendered by surrendering to birth, as opposed to the fixity of 'being born'. In the fourth, I show how the factical infinitude of birth accords with Gebser's understanding of 'the itself', in order to demonstrate the relevance of the traditional concept of the individual's divinity to the project of *Ever-Present Origin*. In the fifth, I compare Gebser's surrender of the problem of birth to Meher Baba's concept of 'positive forgetfulness', exploring how creativity is correlative to non-reactive awareness of the fact of birth. In the sixth, I conclude by highlighting the continuity between the individual problem of birth and the general human crisis, arguing for their essential non-difference in the face of universal Reality.

THE PROBLEM OF BIRTH

> *'Ever since I was born'—that since has a resonance*
> *so dreadful to my ears it becomes unendurable.*
> —CIORAN

A problem for whom? Well, for the born. So that from the outset the problem of birth seems paradoxically to recede and engulf everything including all bases for its being a problem in the first place. Like an abyss expanding behind me the more I emerge from it, at once magnifying and cancelling its mystery, a longest tunnel somehow wholly traversed despite still being inside it. Whatever birth's problem, the time for fixing it seems over, or never was. The trouble is too deep, we are too much in it. So one falls into thinking-feeling about the problem, what Cioran, in *The Trouble With Being Born*, says of its putative remedy, suicide: 'It's not worth the bother [...] since you always [*toujours*] kill yourself too late'.[1] Birth is not worth troubling over, since—ever since I was born— you are always born, too late, everyday. And as the thought of suicide, so ordinary and intolerable, to the point that suicide itself— like the second bullet Carlo Michelstaedter fires into his head[2]— is only a flight from suicide, so the thought of birth escapes itself into the monstrous simplicity of being born, the idiot happiness of the birthday, only to seek secret refuge in some form of forever or never having been.

---

1 E M Cioran, *The Trouble With Being Born*, trans. Richard Howard (New York: Seaver, 1976), 32.
2 'If ever there was one who, in Nietzsche's words, was born posthumously it was Carlo Michelstaedter' (Thomas J Harrison, 'The Michelstaedter Enigma,' *Differentia: Review of Italian Thought* 8/9 [1999]: 125).

The problem from this perspective is how to beget the death of birth, how to let life kill it. For that is what it is doing anyway, in the sense that birth is not mysteriously inaccessible but rather too present, too *toujours*. By 'birth' I am now inescapably talking about the (w)hole impossible everything that holds the entire universe in place around the singular finite and absolutely arbitrary pole of you, all that in the evental face of which everyone only throws up their hands and assumes they were, by means of the weirdest possible spontaneous magic, somehow born from and into it.[3] Just as you crave the *new* and the *next* in evasion of this too tremendously new and next NOW, so do you blindly cling to being born to prevent being/doing the birth you are, think I-was-born-and-will-die so as to enshroud in the baby blanket of 'my life' a living origin whose infinite existential force intimately appears too exterior to ever be identical with one's own. And if you do not like hearing it put this way, if you do not approve of being held personally responsible—for everything—then that only proves it. Only one individual, legend has it, was born laughing.[4] All the rest of us wept. And in this the human feels a perverse security, a pseudo-ownership of life, a weird propriety. So that through failure to truly receive it, the

---

3 'To be born is both to be born of the world and to be born into the world' (Maurice Merleau-Ponty, *Phenomenology of Perception*, trans. Colin Smith [London: Routledge, 1962], 527).

4 'Who is there who does not shudder at the thought of returning to infancy; if the choice had to be made between this and death, who would not choose to die? Yet, this very infancy, beginning life, as it does, not with laughter but tears, is a kind of prophecy, for all its ignorance, of the way of woe upon which it has entered. The only new-born baby that ever laughed, they say, was Zoroaster; but what woe that monstrous laugh portended!' (Augustine, *City of God*, trans. Gerald G Walsh and Daniel J Honan, 3 vols [New York: Fathers of the Church, 1954], XXI.14).

wisdom of Silenus—that it is best not to be born—is passed down, from no one to no one, all in the interest of being someone! And behind it all the nagging sense and strange blind certainty that I am still not born enough, that something more myself than me is yet to be born, even if it turns out to be nothing, nothing but my own inexistence. But I *was* born, wasn't I?

EVER-PRESENT BIRTH

> *For we know that the whole creation*
> *groans and labors with birth pangs*
> *together until now.* —Romans, 8:22

'A body came into the world', says the Schopenhaurian sage Vernon Howard, 'but it wasn't you.'[5] Encountering *Ever-Present Origin* for the first time, and with the question of birth in mind, I come to the conclusion that Gebser would agree with this statement as an articulation of 'self-transparency' (531), and furthermore, that the book overall is an exercise in positively negating birth, as per Cioran's circumspection of being born as ur-attachment: 'If attachment is an evil, we must look for its cause in the scandal of birth, for to be born is to be attached. Detachment then should apply itself to getting rid of the traces of this scandal, the most serious and intolerable of all.'[6] But rather than erasing birth, or attempting to subtract it from life (which must only fail before the limit of birth's fact), *Ever-Present Origin* effectively births the death of birth, bringing

---

5 Vernon Howard, *Your Power of Natural Knowing* (New Life Foundation, 1995), 164.
6 E M Cioran, *Trouble with Being Born*, 19. Page references throughout are to Jean Gebser, *The Ever-Present Origin*, trans. Noel Barstad with Algis Mickunas (Athens, Ohio: Ohio University Press, 1985).

the ending of birth forth in a movement of imminent mutation that is itself birthly, being modeled towards the 'nascence of a new world and a new consciousness' (1) in a radically intensive sense, the world-birth of a new integral Now, 'one where origin [...] blossoms forth anew; and one in which the present is all-encompassing and entire' (7). That Gebser's last lecture was entitled with the question 'Death, too, is birth?' (xxii) is a suggestive first sign of the correctness of seeing his project in these terms.

To begin to elaborate this reading, let us first recall the principle of spontaneity or auto-willing (*sua sponte*) as that which mediates between crisis and mutation, 'eventing' birth from its circumstances, and more specifically, as in the doctrine of spontaneous generation, fills the gap from death to birth, between decay and emergence. Gebser writes, 'A true process always occurs in quanta, that is, in leaps [...] in mutations. It occurs spontaneously, indeterminately, and, consequently, discontinuously' (37). Also in the most normal or regular birth process, there is this spontaneous element which enables everything to happen. The moment of birth remains unpredictable and marks the opening of a durational threshold where life must come near the chance of dying and/or killing via its own generation, where process can dangerously go either way. Stillbirth remains mysterious and is termed 'sudden antenatal death syndrome'. As in spontaneous generation, for instance of worms from rotting flesh, birth's spontaneity holds the space of an unaccountable temporal zone of un-life between death and birth. So in *Ever-Present Origin*, the next mutation of consciousness is what cannot be next as such, not something one can properly anticipate or look forward to—despite that being the task of the book. For the mutative advent of the aperspectival must and can only occur in the mode of a birthly leap into a Now that the world itself in in labor for, a present whose absence is increasingly unendurable and whose imminent immanence makes the tiniest sinceness of birth intolerable. The advent of the fourth world is a perilous passage through the 'perspectivistic tunnel vision' (96), our survival of which seems ever more urgent and unlikely due to the narrowing caused by its own excessive growth, 'the hypertrophy of the "I"' (22). '[I]f we do not overcome the crisis it will overcome us; and only someone who has overcome himself is truly able to overcome. Either we will be disintegrated and dispersed, or we must resolve and effect integrality' (xxvii).

More acutely, we must be born via a channel that precisely not *we*, but only *one*, will survive. The crisis is precisely one that *we* cannot survive, just as looking forward to the next mutation is what cannot not be done by the 'undivided, ego-free person [...] who perceives the whole, the diaphaneity present "before" all origin which suffuses everything' (543). As Vernon Howard says, in terms that perfectly reverse the anagogic imminence of the aperspectival, 'Anything you look forward to will destroy you, as it already has'. So Gebser confirms that what man 'can [...] do to bring about this mutation' is a question of 'presentiation', for 'only someone who knows of origin has present—living and dying in the whole, in integrity' (273). Mutation, as birth into the present of what birth itself births, requires being released from what the prospect of birth typically generates in us: expectation—the religion-building blindness wherethrough man, having witnessed the appearance of divinity and felt—in Hölderlin's words via Gebser—the 'eve of time' (102), forgets the 'pre-ligious' truth of that appearance, i.e., the imperative promise of a new life where 'there is no longer heaven or hell, this world or the other, ego or world, immanence or transcendence' (543), and falls into immediate expectation of a second or next manifestation of God/Truth/Reality and life-to-come, a paradise that is not *today*. Working against the error of looking forward to the new age, *Ever-Present Origin* accordingly invokes Walter Tritsch's description of mutation as 'a sudden illumination of a different segment of reality' (40) and warns us directly against failing to nix the next: 'this presence or being present excludes as a contradiction any kind of future-oriented finality [...] The unintentionality and positive lack of design is therefore important as it excludes all utilitarianism and rationally conditioned, essentially perspectival corrections of the possible' (42). And the book follows its own advice, most significantly I think, by 'excluding as a contradiction' birth from its own movement, not leaving it out, but surrendering birth to origin in a manner that cannot be reduced to an intention. *Ever-Present Origin* gives birth back to itself, without thinking about it. Like taking birth, it must do so, inexorably, because birth, being at once a spaceless-timeless event and that which, with inconceivable asymmetry and arbitrariness, fixes being to space and time, is both the impossibility of the aperspectival and the aperspectival itself.

SURRENDERING BIRTH

> *My mother groan'd! my father wept.*
> *Into the dangerous world I leapt.*
> —BLAKE, 'Infant Sorrow'

To surrender is at once to give up and to give over, to both renounce and provide. As such surrender cannot be calculating, because it gives up on, or abandons hope in, what it gives, and thus becomes capable of receiving it for the first time. True surrender is spontaneous and found in the greatest love, whereby one surrenders oneself to the beloved or 'a man lay[s] down his life for his friends' (John 16:13), in true knowledge, in which the identity of being the truth's knower is renounced before the truth itself, as in Gebser's account of verition, in which previous forms of realization and thought are both surpassed and preserved [*Aufhebung*] (503). In fact the verbal root of *spontaneity*, Proto-Indo-European **spend-* (to make an offering, perform a rite, to engage oneself by a ritual act), contains this sense of sacrifice and self-offering, just as we speak of the spontaneous as something 'surrendered to', as to a *whim*. The spontaneity of true process, what enables mutation, is also thus a species of death, of surrendering to the expiration of what is untenable, even if holding on to it would rob one of nothing other than the chance to surrender, as when jumping into the sea. In such situations we say that there is nothing to lose and everything to gain. And that is the secret of even the most seemingly impossible surrender, which by the truth of spontaneity is preserved from being a loss and gains the giver otherwise ungiveable gifts of losing oneself. So spiritual tradition intuits that whatever one authentically surrenders is always returned in some unforeseeable

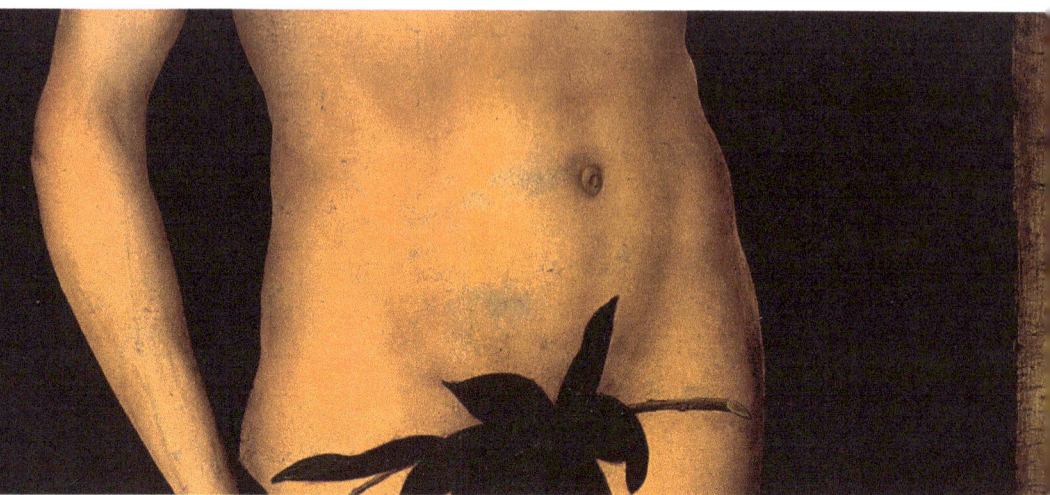

new present, as if never lost. Only a death can give you birth. And if you surrender all, who and what is there to lose, to not possess? As Meister Eckhart says of surrendering to God, 'if a man has gone out of himself in this way, he will truly be given back to himself again […] and all things, just as he abandoned them in multiplicity, will be entirely returned to him in simplicity, for he finds himself and all things in the present "now" of unity'.[7] Likewise the leap of mutation, in the moment of spontaneity, must occur in surrender, by dying to its possibility in midst of entering it most deeply, by leaping at once into and out of the leap. That birth itself is such a mutation is dramatized by the mother who no longer cares about 'giving birth' but knows only the primal urge to 'get this thing out of my body'—a good analogue to the parable about the problem of evil: when the arrow is stuck in you, do you discuss theodicy or find a way to pull it out?

7 Meister Eckhart, *Complete Mystical Works*, trans. Maurice O'C Walshe (New York: Crossroad, 2009), 271.

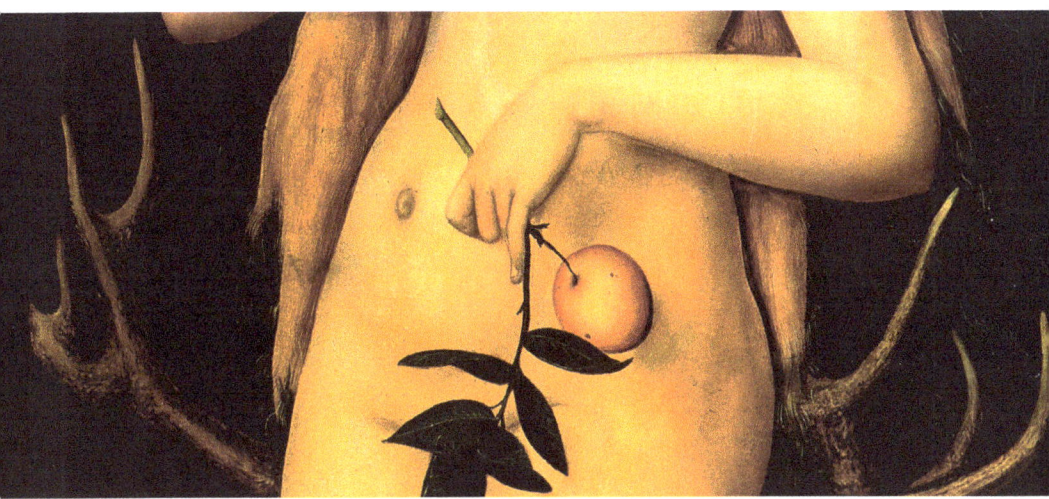

What then does it mean to surrender birth? It means a paradox: that birth is surrendered by surrendering to birth. That is, since one never avoids birth as such, birth is given up by giving in to birth in a way that abandons being born, that surrenders all that is born about one's being. And that is no different from how—as if one is capable of remembering—one is born, in a kind of leap-fall that gives up on by giving in to itself, and vice-versa. One is born by surrendering to birth, and one surrenders to birth, not by wanting it, but by surrendering birth, by giving it up. In other words, *nothing is born without renouncing birth*. Birth takes place in spontaneous surrender of birth. Everyone is born by *not wanting to be*. Upside down. The latent does not properly arrive but as it were falls into presence out of its already being here. So Gebser states that 'far- and deep-reaching mutations […] are latent in origin, they are always back-leaps […] into the *already (ever-)present future*' (530).

The weirdly spontaneous nature of birth may be further clarified by thinking the identity of embodiment and decay, as understood by Plotinus. According to Plotinus, embodiment occurs as the soul's spontaneous generation of a necessary medium for itself: 'In the absence of body, soul could not have gone forth, since there is no other place to which its nature would allow it to descend. Since go forth it must, it will generate a place for itself; at once body, also, exists.'[8] But this only accounts for body, and not the specificity of this body, much less the 'scandal' of the *this* itself, the principle of individuation that makes *Why am I me?* a more unmasterable and terrifying question than *Why is there something rather than nothing?* This demands that we conceive also the negativity of spontaneity, the non-debile inability of the soul to go forth in any other way than the way it does, which places us in the province of decay, where body emerges as a kind of instrumental putrefaction or leakage of soul into form: 'The products of putrefaction are to be traced to the Soul's inability to bring some other thing to being—something in the order of nature, which, else, it would—but producing where it may.'[9] On the one hand the specificity of spatiotemporal emergence is a privation, the prime evil of matter itself, as Pourtless explains: 'Plotinian sensible matter just *is* the *principium individuationis* [...] [it] imposes a veil of obscurity on noetic activity [...] [and] causes an ontological illusion whereby the sensible world and the real are conflated [...] The *principium individuationis* [...] is hence to be identified as primary evil, or evil itself.'[10] On the other hand, the specificity that birth enforces is a

---

8 Plotinus, *Enneads*, trans. Stephen MacKenna (Burdett, New York: Larson, 1992), IV.3.9.
9 Ibid. V.9.14.
10 John A Pourtless, 'Toward a Plotinian Solution to the Problem of Evil', *Aporia* 18 (2008): 13–14.

surplus upon creation, something superadded to being and an immediate sign of the superessential or meta-ontological nature of reality. As Heidegger says of the scholastic understanding of the matter, 'The actualness of the created is not itself actual; it is not itself in need of a coming-to-be or a being-created. Therefore, it may not be said that actuality is something created. It is rather *quid concreatum*, concreated with the creation of a created thing'.[11] Similarly, Gebser's 'concretion of the spiritual' opens 'another world in wait, accessible only through individuation and its supercession' (198). According to Scotus, haecceity or thisness is the very summit of actuality, its ultimate principle: 'this "hecceity" [explains Gilson] is in itself indifferent to both existence and non-existence. It is, in created being, the ultimate determination and actuality which perfects its entity'.[12] Far from being a contingent adjunct of human existence, individuation is for Scotus its divine *raison d'etre*: 'And in those beings which are the highest and most important, it is the individual that is primarily intended by God'.[13] And as Meher Baba makes explicit, individuality is not lost when the drop realizes it is ocean—that is the whole point: 'When the soul comes out of the ego-shell and enters into the infinite life of God, *its limited individuality is replaced by unlimited individuality*. The soul knows that it is God-conscious and thus *preserves its individuality*. The

---

11 Heidegger, *The Basic Problems of Phenomenology*, trans. A Hofstadter (Bloomington: Indiana University Press, 1988), 104.
12 Etienne Gilson, *History of Christian Philosophy in the Middle Ages* (New York: Random House, 1955), 766–67 n 68.
13 John Duns Scotus, *Ordinatio* 11, d.3, n.251, quoted in John Duns Scotus, *Early Oxford Lecture on Individuation*, trans. Allan B Wolter (St. Bonaventure, New York: Franciscan Institute, 2005), xxi.

important point is that individuality is not entirely extinguished, but it is retained in the spiritualised form'.[14]

Such is the genius of individuation, a finitude more infinite than infinity. So the concept of genius itself, originally the god who becomes each man's guardian at the moment of birth, addresses the divine whimsy of individuation. As Agamben observes, in words that may as well be spoken of birth itself, 'One must consent to Genius and abandon oneself to him; one must grant him everything he asks for, for his exigencies are our exigencies, his happiness our happiness. Even if his—our!—requirements seem unreasonable and capricious, it is best to accept them without argument'.[15] In sum, surrendering birth drives one only further into the impossible core of birth itself as the immediate actuality of the *evil genius* of the universe, which is nothing other than the spontaneous decay of divine or superessential Reality into individualized consciousness of itself. For as Meher Baba explains in *God Speaks*, the whole evolutionary and involutionary process of consciousness, which alone generates the messy material world of multifarious forms, hinges on this spontaneity: 'Whatever be the type of gross form and whatever be the shape of the form, the soul spontaneously associates itself with that form, figure, and shape, and experiences that it is itself that form, figure, and shape'.[16] Only spontaneity makes

---

14 Meher Baba, *Discourses*, 6th ed., 3 vols (San Francisco: Sufism Reoriented, 1973), II, 74.
15 Giorgio Agamben, *Profanations*, trans. Jeff Fort (New York: Zone, 2007), 10.
16 Meher Baba, *God Speaks*, 2nd ed. (New York: Dodd & Mead, 1973), 5. Cf. 'Hence when God acquires a particular form, body, or *sharir* according to particular impressions, He feels and experiences Himself as that particular form, body, or *sharir*. God in His stone-form experiences Himself as stone. Accordingly, in consonance with impressions and their consciousness, God feels and

sense of the intuitive dialectic and leapless leap of birth, by which we are placed in the perfect slippage of *this* question and answer: Why am I me? I am not. And only surrendering birth will satis-

experiences that He is metal, vegetation, worm, fish, bird, animal, or human being. Whatever be the type of the gross form and whatever be the shape of the form, the evolving consciousness of God tends God spontaneously to associate Himself with that form, figure, and shape which tends Him to experience Himself through impressions that He is that form, figure, and shape. Similarly, when God is conscious of the subtle body (i.e., the *pran*) then God experiences the subtle world and regards Himself as the subtle body or *pran*. Likewise, God becomes conscious of the mental body (i.e., the *mana* or the mind), experiences the mental world, and regards Himself as the mental body or the *mana* (i.e., the mind). It is only because of impressions that the infinite God, the Over-Soul, without form and infinite, experiences that He is veritably but a finite gross body in the gross sphere (i.e., the *jiv-atma* in *anna bhuvan*), or a subtle body in the subtle sphere (i.e., the *jiv-atma* in *anna bhuvan*), or a mental body in the mental sphere (i.e., the *jiv-atma* in the *mano bhuvan*). God, while experiencing the gross world through gross forms, associates with and dissociates from innumerable gross forms. The association with and dissociation from gross forms are called "birth" and "death", respectively. It is because of impressions that the eternal, immortal, formless God, or the Over-Soul, without births and deaths, has to experience births and deaths a number of times. While God has to experience these innumerable births and deaths because of impressions, He has not only to experience the gross world which is finite and therefore false, but together with it He has also to experience its happiness and misery, its virtue and vice. All forms, figures, and shapes, all worlds and planes, all births and deaths, all virtue and vice, all happiness and misery, experienced by God, Who is eternal, formless and infinite, are the outcome of impressioned consciousness. Since all impressions are but the outcome of the Nothing that manifested as the Nothingness, it means that whatever God experiences through His evolved consciousness in the gross, subtle and mental worlds is the experience of the Nothing; and as this Nothing by nature is nothing, therefore all the experiences in the intermediary illusory states of God are nothing but literally illusion and, as such, false and finite. Only when the impressioned consciousness is freed from all impressions is liberation or *mukti* in human form attained as *nirvana* or *fana*, where only consciousness "Is" and where all else of the Nothing, which was as Nothingness, vanishes forever' (154–55).

fy the terrible desire which birth's abyss endlessly generates: 'Ever since birth, we have been seeking one night to walk together side by side, even if only for a moment in time. Our age is infinity'.[17]

SEPARATED AT BIRTH

> *Two minutes after I was born*
> *I had already lost my beginnings.*
> —CLARICE LISPECTOR

Ever-Present Origin seems to say almost nothing about birth, much less give voice to the horror of individuation which it incites, the dark ground of the terrible need to break out of being. As Levinas explains, 'escape is the need to get out of oneself, that is, to break that most radical and unalterably binding of chains, the fact that the I [*moi*] is oneself [*soi-même*] [...] It is being itself or the "oneself" from which escape flees, and in no wise being's limitation. In escape the I flees itself, not in opposition to the infinity of what it is not or of what it will not become, but rather due to the very fact that it is or that it becomes'.[18] Overall the book appears to stand peacefully outside the pain of this imprisoning interstice and instead adopts an objectivist and collectivist perspective on the evolution of consciousness and human identity, situating itself *vis-à-vis* the universality of mankind and the generic episteme of the human 'we'. *Ever-Present Origin* addresses above all *our* crisis, the crisis of the mutable world we happen to inhabit. From this perspective, it addresses more the *what* of things and does not give voice

---

17 Robert Desnos, *Mourning for Mourning* (London: Atlas Press, 1992), 50. I thank Alina Popa for leading me to this passage.
18 Emmanuel Levinas, *On Escape*, trans. Bettina Bergo (Stanford: Stanford University Press, 2003), 55.

to the radical negativity of the *thatness* of existence, the hyper-individualized factical intensity that remains definitionally beyond the purview of scientific rationalism whose consequentializing of all phenomena, as Gebser observes in connection with the 'consistently overlooked' 'dividing aspect inherent in *ratio*' (95), abandons the measure of origin, the immediate mystery of one's whence and whither, and so becomes the gateway of 'demonic forces' (97).

But as this instance critically intimates, *Ever-Present Origin*, precisely by ordering itself towards a 'time-free present […] as real and efficacious a time-form as those that have preceded it' (543), also continually breaks out of the spatiotemporal perspectivity of historical and plural humanity, all the while preserving it as the last-most form which the new mutation of consciousness will yet contain. So does it repeatedly lay emphasis upon the individual, you, as the someone or anyone who must live the book's truth and realize integrality by 'renounc[ing] the exclusive claim of the mental structure' (529) and surrendering to the 'origin from which every moment of our lives draws its substance' (530), the immanent aperspectival reality, denial of which is tantamount to denying one's own real and ineradicable self. Addressing the originary non-opposition or wholeness encompassing life and death as two poles of the unitary soul, Gebser thus corrects the idealist and materialist positions as follows:

> Enlightened rationalists will not take this potency seriously, while idealist will perhaps find it amusing. It is possible, of course, to ridicule and deride all of this. But anyone who does so is ridiculing his own soul and deriding what he or she cannot fathom and consequentially denies; and such de-

nial is only the result of a lack of courage and strength for another kind of measurement, the contemplation appropriate to the nature of the soul [...] Idealists and materialist are both like two children on a seesaw [...] Each thinks that his own weight and strength is decisive, and neither considers the fulcrum in the middle which, from its point of rest, is what makes their movement and the game itself possible at all. (213)

The passage is particularly significant in regards to birth because it shows how the issue of birth is a kind of non-non-issue for Gebser, one resolved in the immanent life of the integral soul, an entity that need not ever be concerned about its individuation and is thus free to ignore the apparent fact of its specific birth. *Vis-à-vis* the life-death poles of the soul, birth is simply a shadow-image of their unitive point, a hole that only demonstrates the whole. Here there is a move toward the radical truth of facticity that for Meister Eckhart places the individual, as a real eternal unity, above its own creation or beyond origin: 'I once thought—it was not long ago—that I am a man is something other men share with me [...] but that *I am*, that belongs to no man but myself, not to a man, not to an angel, not even to God except insofar as I am one with Him'.[19] The fact of one's being simply is divine, beyond assertion and denial. As Meher Baba says, 'Philosophers, atheists and others may affirm or refute the existence of God, but as long as they do not deny their very existence, they continue to testify their belief in God; for I tell you with divine authority that God is Existence, eternal and infinite. He is everything. For man, there is only one aim in life,

---

19 Meister Eckhart, *Complete Mystical Works*, 131.

and that is to realize his unity with God'.[20] Such is the non-generated and self-original *fact of oneself* next to which birth is an illusion of space-time. Again Eckhart: 'for my essential being is above God [...] For in that essence of God in which God is above being and distinction, there I was myself and knew myself so as to make this man. Therefore I am my own cause according to my essence, which is eternal, and not according to my becoming, which is temporal. Therefore I am unborn, and according to my unborn mode I can never die'.[21] Gebser's term for the *I* that can say this, that can speak its own individuation without recourse to spatio-temporal contextualization is *the itself*, the real species of the human, 'which pervades or "shines through" everything in which the diaphanous spirituality, in its originary presence, is able to become transparent' (135), the ever-new singular one that sublates the I–We or ego-collective dichotomy. So the final chapter of *Ever-Present Origin* cites the Christian apocryphal passage (a mashup of John 15:19 and Ephesians 1:4), 'I have chosen you before the earth began' (542).

At the same time, Gebser's 'waring' of the integral fulcrum of experience moves not towards transcendent unborn identity but into a sense of the profoundly participatory nature of being, according to which it is impossible to claim anything as one's own, even and especially oneself. If in one direction the aperspectival event of oneself opens into the view of birth as too absent, in the other direction it opens onto the view of birth as too present, as too common to be bothered about as such. Such is the view that renders one indifferent to the fact of birth because there can only

---

20 *Lord Meher*, 4055, http://www.lordmeher.org.
21 Meister Eckhart, *Complete Mystical Works*, 424.

be, as Meher Baba says, 'one real birth and one real death'[22] and all the births and deaths we perceive around us, including our current physical birth around which we see at best darkly, are *mere* births and deaths, passing forms and modifications of the drop-soul or individualized ocean as it swims like a worm from and into itself along the evolutionary path. What is the significance of earthly birth (or death) in the face of the vast Reality one's very being born from-into itself manifests an absolute indissolubility? And if you consider yourself to be only an epiphenomenon, a random creation of a universe that somehow would exist without you, or more biologically, a walking corpse hallucinating that it is alive, then the matter of one's birth only diminishes further in significance. As that which, par excellence, you cannot take credit for, except in a manner that would cancel the contingency of birth, birth is the abyss wherein one is always already eternally married to the Real, even if it turns out, by some tremendous twist, to be nothing at all. Either way, birth is not what makes oneself. Befitting Gebser's etymological gloss of *individuum* as 'someone divided and dividing by seeing' (182 n 6), your birth is simply something that separated you at birth.

UNREMEMBERING BIRTH

> There is one real birth and one real death. You are born once, and you really die only once. What is the real birth? It is the birth of a drop in the ocean of reality. What is meant by the birth of a drop in the ocean of reality? It is the advent of in-

22 *Lord Meher*, 4388.

dividuality, born of individuality through a glimmer of the first most-finite consciousness, which transfixed cognizance of limitation into the unlimited. What is meant by the real death? It is consciouness getting free of all limitations. Freedom from all limitations is real death. It is really the death of all limitations. It is Liberation. In between the real birth and the real death, there is no such reality as the so-called births and deaths. What happens in the intermediate stage known as births and deaths is that the limitations of consciousness gradually wear off, until consciousness is free of limitations. Ultimately, consciousness, totally free of limitations, experiences the unlimited reality eternally.[23]

It is in the scope of such a vista upon the advancing stream of consciousness that *Ever-Present Origin* practices and requires of its reader what may be termed a *positive forgetfulness* of birth. As defined by Meher Baba, 'The whole philosophy of approaching and realizing the Truth hinges on the question of what we may call forgetfulness [...] positive forgetfulness is one in which the mind remains aware of external stimuli, but refuses to react to them. The negative forgetfulness is either mere unconsciousness—a stopping of the mind as in sound sleep—or an acceleration of it as in madness, which has been defined as a way of avoiding the memory of suffering.'[24] Applying the principle to birth brings into relief the pervasive negative forgetfulness which conditions the general human attitude, flipping between taking birth's event totally for granted—'I'm here, now what?'—and using it as excuse/justification for

---

23 *Lord Meher*, 4388.
24 Meher Baba, *God Speaks*, 213.

doing whatever: *I was born*, it's *my* life, happy birthday to *me*. To positively forget birth, alternately, implies a full awareness of its phenomenon that neither disregards birth's significance nor dramatizes it around the separative or secondary center of 'that which has been born'. Here we should not fail to remember that, despite the discrediting of creationism, we (culturally speaking) still conceive of ourselves as effects of the universe, emergent things produced by some ungraspable reality yet somehow deserving of operatively being our own centers of the universe.[25] As if *I* can effect integrality! Positive forgetfulness, contrariwise, implies the avenue of a creative neutrality towards the fact of birth, an attitude that would neither appropriate nor ignore its inevitable force or spontaneous imperative, a being-in-but-not-of birth. The creative capacity of positive forgetfulness is described by Meher Baba as follows:

> In such moments of true forgetfulness there is a mental detachment from all material surroundings in which the poet allows his imagination to soar. An artist, when he gives form to an ideal in which he completely forgets himself and all irrelevant surroundings, creates a masterpiece. The best of philosophy is uttered when a man surveys the problem of life without reference to the ups and downs of his purely personal circumstances; and some of the greatest scientific discoveries have been made in this same frame of mind. Such manifestations of genuine spontaneity of forgetfulness are very rare indeed, and although it is said that poets, artists and philosophers are born and not made, these fleet-

---

25 See Nicola Masciandaro, 'Mysticism or Mystification?: Against Subject-Creationism', *English Language Notes* 50 (2012): 253-58.

ing phases of real forgetfulness are the result of efforts made in past lives. (214)

Importantly, the occurrence of positive forgetfulness is itself correlated with the vector of one's birth, suggesting furthermore that significant human creativity, which Gebser describes in terms of 'the way origin, budding and unfolding in space and time, emerges on earth and in our daily lives' (530), is not only essentially more connected than we may directly perceive with pre-birth latencies, with something still-to-be-born via birth, but furthermore, that the spontaneity of positive forgetfulness in general is non-incidentally linked to birth specifically, that *non-reactive awareness of birth is the paradigm of positive forgetfulness.* That is, not only does true, creative detachment necessarily involve self-detachment in the mode of non-identification with oneself as born, but positive forgetfulness of birth itself, alertly acute awareness of birth's fact that yet refuses to freeze into reaction, is an essential mode of spontaneous creativity. Here we may notice the phenomenal resonance between birth as spontaneous association of consciousness with new form and creativity as self-forgetful production. Of course to be true to this source will entail not following its consequences past itself. So here let me quickly kill in utero a potential pep talk on forgetful birth-awareness as the great untapped resource of human potential. Instead we must here think birth, not only as not properly an opportunity for something else, but as *an opportunity for nothing except not itself.* Birth is the chance—thank God!—to *not,* to never ever be born. To stop counting on something else to do it for you and die *now,* while you still have a chance. To exit the world in which you are trapped by entering it for real, from the outside. As Meher Baba said in 1926, on the occasion of his brother's death: 'The joy expressed by people at the birth of a child should be expressed when a person breathes his last—instead of all the show of sorrow, grief, and sympathy. This is sheer ignorance and those who understand the secret of birth and death feel sorry at this hypocritical pretense […] Die such a death that you will not have to die again. Die, all of you, in the real sense of the word so that you may live ever after.'[26] The imperative of birth, heard by everyone and obeyed by few, is thus a kind of autophagic or self-eating command, an instruction authentically followed by not following it, only by listening to it, too clearly, to the point of forgetting that one is listening, forgetting in the listening that one is born, knowing in the forgetting that one is not. May what birth whispers from inside your ear be the death of you! Like the child who is father of the man, birth commands what parents instinctively want for their children. With spontaneous love, birth tells you, whatever you do, do not be like *me*. But humans have the hardest time following even the simplest instructions.

BIRTH TOLD ME TO

> Event of oneself, ongoing primordial,
> Without way or opening, a very hard fall.
> In the beginning, beginning's very middle,
> See my blinding opening, your pure white hole.
> Summoned by something making answering its call,
> Walking an opening where stepping is trail.

26 *Lord Meher*, 643.

Stumbling perfectly, on stumbling, the way a ball,
Deep surface, no opening, feels, cannot, its roll.
Will these clauses, unconcluding, speak being's wheel,
Our anarchic opening, foundation beyond frail?
Or are they, caught underneath, wax to empty seal,
Signs only of opening, of depths unreal?
Event of oneself, so perversely actual,
Queerest opening, a sparrow through the hall.

The imperative of *Ever-Present Origin* is clear: we can do this the easy way or we can do it the hard way. Sooner or later, with a lesser or greater share of self-created suffering, the new mutation of consciousness, an integral reality, will be realized. 'There can be no question that our task will be resolved, since it originates in necessity. The only open question is whether it will be resolved soon' (539). This is a pandemic pregnancy, in which the pervasiveness of crisis *proves* the necessity of mutation or emergence of a new whole. As Meher Baba put it: 'The condition of the world, the strife and uncertainty that is everywhere, the general dissatisfaction with and rebellion against any and every situation shows that the ideal of material perfection is an empty dream and proves the existence of an eternal Reality beyond materiality.'[27] The imperative of mutation, its *must*, is of a piece with crisis, and hiddenly *is* it—mutation being precisely not the order of a remedy for the crisis, but the necessary leap into a new sphere. 'The new world culture', Meher Baba

---

27 Meher Baba, *The Everything and the Nothing* (Beacon Hill, Australia: Meher House Publications, 1963), 55.

says, '*must* emerge from an integral vision of truth.'[28] Critically, by virtue of the inevitability of this necessity, inseparable from the very unity of life, that which maieutically effects this new mutation is not on the level of escape or emergency response. 'The spiritual experience that is to enliven and energise the New Humanity cannot be a reaction to the stern and uncompromising demands made by the realities of life [...] *Man will be dislodged again and again from his illusory shelters by fresh and irresistible waves of life, and will invite upon himself fresh forms of suffering by seeking to protect his separative existence through escape.*'[29] What we must grasp, then, in order to realize this imperative, is the sheer vertiginous non-difference between self- and world-transformation, between the abiding experience that will enliven the new integral humanity and the aperspectival culture that shall characterize it. In Vernon Howard's terms, 'To live in another world, be another world'.[30] And it is precisely the incident of human birth, that spontaneous aperspectival flash wherethrough you leapt into world and world sprang from you, which best instructs us in this non-difference, providing a retroactive foretaste of the birth to come, a to-come that yet is only to be realized today. Natality is not futural but directed to the now. Birth's vector is from and towards the principle of why and how you are here, all the more insistently as 'I should not be here' is the very cry of birth. As Meher Baba explained on the occasion of his birthday in 1937:

---

28 Meher Baba, *Listen Humanity*, narrated and ed. D E Stevens (New York: Harper Colophon, 1967), 142, my italics.
29 Meher Baba, *Discourses*, I, 21.
30 Vernon Howard, *Cosmic Command* (Pine: Arizona, 1979), #1243.

The incident of birth is common to all life on earth. Unlike other living creatures which are born insignificantly, live an involuntary life, and die an uncertain death, the physical birth of human beings connotes an important and, if they are extra circumspect about it, perhaps a final stage of their evolutionary progress. Here onward, they no longer are automatons but masters of their destiny which they can shape and mold according to will. And this means that human beings, having passed through all the travails of lower evolutionary processes, should insist upon the reward thereof, which is 'Spiritual Birth' in this very life, and not rest content with a promise in the hereafter.[31]

Who brought you to this point? How did you make it into this form? All I know for certain is that I should not be here. That this world, this time, this space, this self…is not my home. To listen to birth with such circumspection, to open your ears to the uncanny silence of its aperspectival spiral, means to recoil on yourself in a very special way, abandoning hope in what the world might give a *you* who never was and is already dead. To understand this *should* signifies to groan in the voice of that hearing, to die immortally into that mystical birth which lurks so near in the acosmic core of this world, deeper than all lust and longing, inside the abyss of spontaneous loving surrender. I will therefore conclude by recalling Meister Eckhart's perfectly human description of this birth:

---

31 *Lord Meher*, 1788.

> [T]he masters write that in the very instant the material substance of the child is ready in the mother's womb, God at once pours into the body its living spirit which is the soul, the body's form. It is one instant, the being ready and the pouring in [...] You need not seek Him here or there [...] No need to call to Him from afar: He can hardly wait for you to open up. He longs for you a thousand times more than you long for Him: the opening and the entering are a single act.[32]

---

32 Meister Eckhart, *Complete Mystical Works*, 58.

Rokujō

appears

cinnabar
n'blo

murasaki
gold

turquoise

The Philosophy of the Flowers

In Search for the Genealogy of Yūgen—A Cosmic Sublime

ELISABET YANAGISAWA

Never forget the beginner's mind.
—ZEAMI MOTOKIYO (1363–1443)

¶ IN MY WORK as a conceptual artist, I crave an unmediated view of material reality, a sensible awareness of an immanent life that lies beyond the visual surface commonly projected as a commercial image. I adhere to a form of artistic practice where the categorical division between life and art dissolves, and by so doing develops a renewed relationship to ethics and aesthetics with an understanding of how they might work in tandem. In this way, the two become a relation deriving their meaning from within each other, yet one that is not about forming a subjectivity or an eccentric ego. This may sound threatening for some, but this phenomenon is not about returning to a conservative concept of beauty in search of ideals and transcendence.

My thinking is much more concrete, and departs from the Deleuzian immanent *field of consistency*. It is about capturing a pre-subjectivity of an impersonal and differentiated subject through the attention of sensible perception, a mode of receptive *singularity* that is simultaneously a part of the unity of social and cosmic perspective. For me, cosmic means something that has a potential to be something we do not grasp totally; it concerns other scales, is multidimensional and amazing in its unfathomable embodiment. The key to understanding this embodiment is to re-examine our notion of presence in the context of dwelling.

This thinking is close to what Félix Guattari develops in *Three Ecologies*, where he uses the term 'eco' referring to the Greek etymology *oikos*, meaning home. Home exists on different scales as a 'home' for the self to dwell. The spatiality of home can be a materialistic place, a bird-nest for the soul, or a place to swathe the body in a support like swaddling a newborn. On a gradient scale, cloth is a dwelling, the next layer is a room, then a house. Then come the urban or rural walls, floors and scaffoldings of the city.

My life world depends on these tectonics, concrete vertical upholders of my space, supporters of my inner layers, my unseen interiority and invisibility, and the mental singularity of it all. In the paradoxically light and simultaneously arduous way of listening to the senses, we recreate ourselves in an ongoing sensible process as an ethico-aesthetical resingularization. From the concrete, I become an abstraction. I do not become an abstraction from a conceptualization, but from a spatial awareness.

I

MANY YEARS AGO I received a small piece of paper from a ninety-year-old ikebana master,[1] Arai sensei. I came to know him briefly in

---

1 Ikebana is the art of flower arrangement, including the act of cutting as well as the sculptural installation of living plants.

Tokyo when I visited my aunt. Arai sensei was her teacher in ikebana who came from a family of ikebana teachers deriving from the seventeenth century. I joined them both to visit an ikebana exhibition where my aunt and Arai sensei presented their ikebana in the simple tea-style: a single flower in a vase. Compared to the extravagant and gorgeous contemporary styles, their installation radiated a profound simplicity. After the exhibition opening, we rested at a bench in a temple courtyard where Arai sensei gave me a piece of paper. He had written the characters 幽玄 (*yūgen*), a concept which has since stood at the core of my artistic repertoire. This piece of paper became a ticket to an aesthetic-philosophical journey into pre-modern Japanese philosophy; a gateway allowing me to see places, encounter artists, and touch rare items.

Today the character *yūgen*, as used in Japanese aesthetics, connotes a meaning close to 'the beautiful sublime', defined as dim, weak, faint, and indistinct. It is an immanence that departs from the real concreteness of physicality, sliding from invisibility to visibility as a layered transversal in the betweenness of the real and the phantasm. The first symbol 幽 (*yū*) encompasses a range of meanings: darkness and confinement; a spiritual relation to ghosts, spirits and other worlds; imprisonment; mystery; quiet places, solitude and secluded things; deep water; cosmos; and a cosmic sublime. The character 玄 (*gen*) originally described a dark, profound, tranquil colour of the universe.[2]

The concept of *yūgen* derives from Taoism, with roots as far back as the tenth century. *Yūgen* is linked to the feminine prin-

---

[2] Andrew Nathanael Nelson, *The Modern Reader's Japanese-English Character Dictionary* (Rutland, Vermont: Charles E Tuttle, 1962).

ciple of *yin* in the philosophy of continuous cyclic change. *Yin* is receptivity and openness, but is also a closure, a spatial womb, an inner cosmic realm. The philosophy of *yin-yang* is about inter-related polar forces in a mode of continuous transition. Neither force dominates the other; each are reciprocally interconnected in a fluid penetration of their reality. *Yin-yang* enhances no static ideal; stillness signifies death, and animation life.

Zeami

It was in my *yūgen* research that I first came in contact with Noh. My presumption about Noh was that it is an elegant and luxurious classical art form. How wrong I was! Noh was brought to its creative height in the fourteenth–fifteenth centuries by the actor and writer Zeami Motokiyo (1363–1443). He wrote sixteen treatises on the secrets of the art of Noh for actors/artists.[3] In his essay *Fushikaden* (The Philosophy of The Flowers), Zeami developed the notion of *yūgen* through metaphorical images describing a graded advancement into the sublime via nine stages.[4] The 'flower' is a metaphor of the aesthetic level, the intersection of inner imaginary tension and external form. This performative expression reaches higher and higher degrees of *yūgen*.

Written sometime between 1400 and 1418, *Fushikaden* became an exclusive guide to life for Zeami's acting troupe. It remained secret for a long time in Japan until the latter part of the nine-

---

3 *The Flowering Spirit: Classic Teachings on the Art of Nō*, trans. William Scott Wilson (Tokyo: Kodansha, 2006).
4 The nine stages of *yūgen* are described in detail in Makoto Ueda, 'Zeami on the Art of the Nō Drama: Imitation, *Yūgen* and Sublimity', in *Japanese Aesthetics and Culture: A Reader*, ed. Nancy G Hume (Albany: SUNY, 1995).

teenth century, when Fushikaden gradually made its way into the hands of the general public. Although *Fushikaden* is about Noh drama, Zeami's writings are about artistic practice and his general philosophical outlook on the art of life. Zeami's main intention was to create a multisensible art form by sliding from concrete to abstract as a transformation of human conditions between the real and abstract.

Noh theatre developed among illiterates in small fishing villages under the guidance of Zeami's teachings. The artists/villagers dedicated their talents completely to performing this drama by playing multiple roles in the production: musicians, members of the choir, actors, costume-makers, and carpenters. No one directed; the work was created collectively. During the last years of his life, Zeami was sent to the island of Sado in political exile. The reason why is still unclear. The feudal government exiled many who posed a threat, such as intellectuals, aristocrats, court-people, priests, and monks. On the island of Sado, they earned their keep working in a goldmine: the source of most Japanese gold. These exiles intermingled with native fishing villages, and a highly cultivated composite community developed.

Noh in Tokyo

The *devise*—'don't forget the beginner's mind'—resounded in my mind when I attended a staged Noh performance for the first time. I let myself be immersed in impressions without trying to read the plot beforehand. The plot was completely subordinated by a personal floating experience affected by concrete impressions.

I was a pendulum shifting between two different modes. One

was the present moment sitting in a chair in the hall enjoying a play at a theatre. The other was more abstract; I was intensely drawn into a dreamlike atonal atmosphere, a floating phantasmatic experience that totally outstripped me. The harsh sound of the choir and the shakuhachi flute pressed me into a narrow confined passage. I was there, present, and simultaneously in an abstract world. This subversive, encompassing feeling was textured and had a dissonant spatiality, yet perfectly in order, refined, reduced, almost stripped to a naked rawness.

I tried not to analyse how the multisensible setting could produce this atmosphere, so I made notes. I rapidly sketched in my notebook throughout the four-hour play in a half-sleeping state. Was this an act of writing matter into time? The black pen-lines became an airy inscription faintly touching the cream paper of the notebook; compilations of animated tropes emerged as gestures scripted over the surface—what I later tried to transform to verbal language:

> *A narrow-striped tea-colored kimono enters the stage. The bare-head man turns around towards the eight-men choir-composition with black, narrow shoulders and 90-degree sleeves. The costume of the village man is unfinished, a wrinkled tangle of indefinite pleats flow out on the floor. The voices from the choir sound in eightfold dislocations: tone shifts and temporal shifts. My sound sketches look like a vibration. A man is now sitting in the foreground, a form consisting of solid lightness, a green grey drop turns to the front and creases in the bend of the arm concealing fingertips in the*

mass of cloth. The shakuhachi player⁵ sitting straight in front with black shoulders, shoulder line slithered, holds the flute across sleeves falling in straight diagonals a shoulder width's distance of displacement edgeways. A light shift in height, the heavy sleeve slants and exposes big open dark folds, light-lined slots on vertical lines hang down towards the light hakama.⁶ The shakuhachi player becomes a floating sculpture. His head, with hair cut short, accentuates the deep falls of the kimono sleeves. He sits straight upon the floor. The wide trousers are floating out in a contained form. Yaooo...yaooo...yaooo...

On Sado Island

It was a chilly day in October when I travelled to Sado Island to carry out genealogic research into the notion of *yūgen*. A childhood friend of my uncle's was living on the island. He was a building contractor with a great interest in arts and crafts, and he had arranged for me to meet Kondo-san, a Noh-player. For one intense day, Kondo-san guided me around the island. Kondo was a slim and distinct man in his fifties, but had the appearance of a young boy. He was dressed in a subdued outfit of light grey wool and carried a leather shoulder bag across his breast. He spoke only Japanese in a modulated, gentle voice that almost sounded like singing—clear and alert. I could not grasp the whole of what he said, but his body talked to me, and he vigorously moved around me, his voice reverberating in the empty performance spaces of our visit. I felt comfortable, undistracted, and experienced a mood of

---

5 Shakuhachi is a wooden flute with a sibliant, hoarse sound.
6 Hakama is a long culotte with broad pleats.

defocused concentration that was able to effortlessly perceive all spatial encounters.⁷

We did not know each other personally, but I felt at home in the open outdoor settings he took me to. Every place was an empty stage consisting of a floor and roof, but no walls. Pillars of cedar held up the thick, massive cedar floorboards from the ground. The Noh-stage has no decoration: the people in the audience are supposed to create their own backdrop image in their minds. Kondo told me historical anecdotes, which I could not fully follow, but his rhyming and rhythmic voice accompanied my 'touchings'; my fingertips caressed the gravity of the pillars, my feet touched the empty floors, and I moved unplanned, defocalized and joyous.

Behind the stage was the mirror room where the actor transformed himself into the role he was supposed to play. Kondo moved lightly and pointed to an imaginary mirror. Gazing into the mirror, he directed his mind to the spirits for assistance in visualizing the role behind the mask. This act is the emergence of one's becoming; it is the embodied spirit or invisibility disguised by the mask. Embodied invisibility was to be perceived in the form of the performance through the player's posture (*kata*) and movements, which together created an atmospheric suspension of *yūgen*. This interstice, a place and a potential site of spatio-temporal in-between-ness, is the Japanese notion of *ma*. I asked Kondo to tell me more about *ma*.

---

7 Defocused concentrtion, or defocalizing, is a term to describe a kind of seeing or perceiving with the senses in an altered perspective than focal gazing. The term is used by Jeremy Narby, *The Cosmic Serpent: DNA and the Origins of Knowledge* (New York: Jeremy P Tarscher/Putnam, 1998). 'To let the eyes go as if you are looking through the book without seeing it. Relax into the blur and be patient'. Narby compared this mode with a Bourdieu's phrase 'to objectify one's objectifying relationship'.

Ma is a concept of negative space, an 'in-between-ness' in both spatial and temporal fields. While the Japanese character for *ma*, 間, looks like an empty house, the suggestion is that this emptiness is everything because it exists in relation to different entities. Not only that, but because it is relational, it is active. This emptiness of no-space is a potential to be filled, moved, or opened. Thus, emptiness is a possibility to unfold.

In Noh, spatial *ma* is used to emphasize interruptions in order to invigorate a form or an act bringing emphasis to a gesture. *Ma* creates an intense physical suspension of movement in the air through a subtle shifting of a posture made in slow motion followed by a sudden, fast, subversive turnover of gesture to shift the viewer's imagination of setting. Determined and powerful, the actor moves in a precise direction. The temporal *ma* is the gap between tones: a pause, a standstill, or an untimely state of freeze. This empty temporal space punctuates the rhythms of the performance; it is the place where atonal vocal tunes slide. Dissonant tones intermingle in *ma*, each tone with a singularity in its own vibration. What I begin to perceive here is a multitude of crossings with voice and gesture in the sea of in-between-ness.

The next morning, Kondo and I met at the Shou-Hou Temple in middle of the island, and I asked him to tell me more about *genzai* Noh and *mugen* Noh. He smiled. We shared a mutual understanding of these concepts; *genzai* means visible, apparent, while *mugen* means invisible, with an inner tension. As I gradually began to understand these crucial Noh concepts more fully, I saw how the notions of *genzai* and *mugen* are interrelated as if juxtaposed on a gliding scale with gradual change. Things turned from invisibility to visibility—and the reverse. But I felt I was too eager; I had to carefully notice his way of teaching and not diverge.

He had already planned the day; we were supposed to have a meeting with a Zen priest. Kondo brought me into the temple, and we met Yachida-sama, a tall man dressed in a black kimono. Kondo talked and moved easily in the temple space, I went around and watched how carefully Yachida-sama had arranged disparate things. He was like an artist making his installations of small, precious objects and flowers in the temple hall. At first I did not really understand why we were there, until I learned that Yachida-sama was especially interested in Noh. We waited there for a while until the priest brought forth an old box in Paulownia-wood.[8] He carefully opened the lid and unwrapped a mask. Zeami had been its owner. A short tale of twin baby-boys was written in ink on the patched silk cloth and calligraphy writing stained the nude wood on the inside of the mask. Slowly, Yachida-sama told us the story about the babies who died.

Without the slightest trace of sentimentality, Yachida-sama carefully handled the box, the cloth, and the mask to us. He did not attempt to please us, nor to show us anything special. This was a bare presentation, a rawness of presence with no subjective preposition. There was an air of impersonal affection: a tender matter of factness. When we rose to leave, the priest briefly said to me:

> Noh is about transforming the concrete into abstract; everything moves through the five senses.

I understood entirely what he meant. Later we entered Kondo-

---

8 Paulownia (Japanese: *kiri*) wood is very light, fine-grained, soft and warp-resistant. It is used for chests and boxes

san's kimono shop and stepped up to the third floor. The ferry was scheduled to leave, and we were in a hurry. Rectangular, flat kimono boxes were piled on the floor. Hastily, but very carefully, he opened one box after the other to show me his treasures, an abundance of ancient kimonos and textiles. The kimonos and the artefacts were in an orderliness. He handled his belongings with reverence for the materials. Kondo next opened a box with a white wooden mask inside. He took it out and threaded a purple silk ribbon through the holes at the sides and dressed me in a heavy antique Noh robe. Looking into the mirror, I saw a stranger. I was gazing through the hollows of a mask of a young girl. The unfolding of these textile treasures gave me a feeling of an urgent act, a condensed compression. But why this now? The ferryboat would not wait. We had to move on.

The very last place Kondo wanted to show me was the Noh headquarters. Nobody was there, but Kondo had the key. He wanted to tell me this was an exception as women were not allowed to enter this stage. Nobody would know. We stepped on the *hanamachi* or 'bridge', a passage from the mirror room to the stage. This was the passage between different planes; the imaginary and the real, the dead and the living, the phantasm and the present. The stage was there in a cold darkness, empty. Kondo was now wearing a dark pair of wide trousers, the traditional *hakama* culotte, and posed himself in a *kata* or 'posture'. The scene was subdued, no lights were on, and I scarcely saw his contour. Slowly, Kondo directed himself with his whole body into a *ma*. Suddenly, he stomped his foot with a distinct gesture onto the massive cedar wood floor. The sound of his walk ebbed away in a ripple, and his motion lingered on in an intensity of emptiness. Decisively, he turned around and disappeared into the passage. I did not follow.

Our last visit was to the Haguro Jinja, the smallest Noh stage on the island built by only fourteen families. It is situated on the fringe of a forest with its back against a steep slope covered by many thousand-year-old cedar trees. It drizzled; the rain fell in a diagonal movement. The empty stage was a similitude of *empty space*. It yawned; its heavy hollow in massive wood was like a wide mouth.

Kondo-san had brought three umbrellas in three different nuances of beige. Simultaneously, Kondo-san, my uncle Kohji, and I moved around the field, unplanned. A mood occurred in this undirected motion, and a kind of neutral ambience surfaced. An intense emotion then grasped me. Seeing them animated like that gave me a detached flash-feeling of my own present plasticity. 'I am spatial', I thought. This almost brought me to experience the ecstasy of emptiness. The ostensibly neutral surface of this ground emerged as a jutting object defined by the composition of the rhythmic sound of rain, the pale light, high cedars, and non-colours upon this no-place. The visible space became a suggestive, vague, pale echo of the gravity of an innate phantasm.

The next day I was supposed to meet the building contractor on the island; his name was Kondo as well. We met him at his ugly office. The interior was a mishmash of different styles from the last four or five decades, and it had the feeling of a forgotten workplace in the countryside, but where big projects were constructed, and money was not lacking. It was not pretending to be something other than this peculiar office. He was a charming old man, wearing a threadbare wool-sweater. To my surprise he said he was the superintendent for the waste gold mine. The office was placed just on the shore of the abandoned mines. We went outdoors, and there I discovered the rusted cranes and rails with hollow carriages—items that still remained on the stone-beach, now a national heritage. I stood in this awkward atmosphere on this shore of nowhere at the foot of a pier pointing out into the wild and foaming Japanese Sea.

Darkness quickly fell. We wiggled our way up the hill to contractor Kondo's summerhouse, a timber *minka* cottage.[9] Led by flaming torches through the pitch-darkness, we entered Kondo's guest-house and met ten villagers, all childhood friends of Kondo, now with white hair. They sat around a fire broiling freshly gathered *Sazae* (abalone, mollusc, sea snails). As Kondo was the village's patron of the arts, he served us handmade *soba* with simple bouillon in big ceramic bowls made by a master potter from the nearby village.

I had a certain feeling of 'no things' in relation to each other: I chewed over the texture of grotesque molluscs in my mouth; benevolent strangers surrounded me speaking in that kind of low-voice that expresses a care for things; and Kondo told his story about how he dove to harvest the sea snails that same morning. This compilation of haptic materials,[10] the pitch-darkness, and this no-plot story all had a strong intensity of reality: an atmospheric setting which suddenly emerged in the lighting of torches. This was no theatre, this was reality invisibly sliding over towards an attuned setting with bodies emerging from the darkness as temporary sketches. As I chewed, a man tossed out my beer and filled my

9 *Minka* is a traditional countryside house built in farmer style with thatched roof and handcrafted in wood.
10 Haptic, from Greek *haptomai*, 'to touch'.

glass with new brew: *Kiomeru*—a Shinto ritual meaning 'starting from zero'. When two people meet for the first time, there should be nothing between them, only clarity.

II

MY FIRST ENCOUNTER with *yūgen* from my readings was about cosmic sublimity. I imagined a dark, elegant void with a ghostly ephemeral presence floating in the sphere. A dissonance—a harsh sound and raw texture—might be present in the assemblage. But after my experiences on Sado Island, these dreamlike phantasms were replaced by a paradoxical spatial awareness. My new connotations were subtler, and more real. This experience of *yūgen* was no longer an archaic concept of beauty. I realized it circumscribes the same reality, the same world that we live in now. All simple and pure encounters with beauty are the same, aren't they? Styles change, materials and space change, many things change, but what remains unchanged? Is there something inherent in human perception itself that is predisposed to valuing these sensible occurrences?

I reread the *Tao Te Ching*,[11] and I tried to recognize some of the sequences from my own spatial experiences in Sado. Yes, it was there, the floating, transgressing, and amorphous feeling of raw space: hollows, empty spaces that embodied potentiality, the emerging, yet not born. Horizontal and open, this was a plane of consistency, nude and pure, which elastically stretched out its vast-

---

11 *Tao Te Ching* can be translated as 'The Book of the Immanence of the Way' or 'The Book of the Way and how it Manifests itself in the World', or simply, 'The Book of the Way'. It was written by Lao-tzu (551–479 BCE).

ness. I agree, this is a feminine spatiality with a proximate scale of sensibility expressed as a fluid motion poured out in a gesture and dissolved. It is a treasure wrapped in an old cloth stained with ink and hidden in a simple box. I drew this space out of a constraint, a shell, touched it with my fingertips, and chewed it in my mouth. The ugly surface lay there beneath a pile of hard shells—remnants. This was similar to the alchemy of scent creation: gruesome substances in encounter with some other ostensible horrible consistency. And the sum of it will become the most subtle and nuanced experience.

Yūgen is an impersonal beauty in its anonymity, never dominating, never using many words. *Yūgen* is disguised as a beggar, an ostensibly poor person, but with incredible artistic skill. This reminds me of Jean Genet's *Aerialist*. Disguised in a raw, trashed, old coat, the high-wire artist hides his nude, slender, beautiful body that is a living artwork in itself. His theatrical moment is in these short ephemeral minutes when he unwraps himself from the ugly garment and enters the rope posing in his moving *kata*. All the tension in his body from years of hard training, all his constraint, is released here onto this rope, this line unto nothingness.

Spatial Awareness

French actor, dramatist, and playwright Antonin Artaud (1896–1948) held a contemporary understanding of Zeami's teachings. He understood *kata* as a strict expression of inner tension and a way to abstract spatiality. In 'Artaud, East and West', his introduction to *Artaud on Theatre*, Brian Singleton writes:

In western theatre, realism, according to Artaud, reflects, describes and most importantly imitates. For the theatre of the East the representation of reality by heavy codified gestures reveals everything about reality which cannot be imitated or described. Artaud refers to the irony in the fact that the surface freedom and spontaneity offered by the western stage is an illusion since it only provides for a material representation of the world. He preferred to manufacture formalism without the raw sociocultural materials to support it. He talks of the potential of eastern theatre to unleash demons through formalized gestural language but does not point out that for a society to perform and unleash them it must first believe in their existence and effect.[12]

When I read this I don't feel alone in my understanding of the importance of the bodily form, the *kata*. Antonin Artaud understood the body as a spatial form, and not anything else. He saw the body as a spatiality that transgresses the viewer's own awareness, thus leading to another level of perception. This is a perception not based on representation, but on structural seeing and experiencing spatiality. In other words, there is a difference between shape and shape, between form and form, even if it all looks the same. The corporeal body does not just appear as a concrete shape, even though it might only look so. The visible contour depends on an *inner tension* that takes place invisibly within a living entity.

Artaud's understanding of Zeami's teachings is that the external is not only a question of shape and expression, but a medium

---

12 Claude Schumacher and Brian Singleton, eds, *Artaud on Theatre* (London: Methuen Drama, 1989).

for us to perceive invisible tensions, if they exist. This has nothing to do with social matters. It has to do with spatial matters and the subtle ways of observing sensibilities that are almost imperceptible. But what is difficult today with this kind of awareness? Isn't it the remark that Singelton makes: to perform and unleash the demons, a society must first believe in their existence and effect. To talk of demons is a way to open the potential for an inner power of tension, a spirituality, a power bigger than the ordinary, the presupposed habitual, the common. This is nothing supernatural, it is immanent and belongs to our potentiality to be receptive, perform, and unleash. In that way, we might see the difference in external effects. This is what we can experience when we really see a touching performance, in whatever art form. And the effect might as well be left in matter only, even in an empty void. This is what inspiration is about: inhaling air and receiving energy. Singleton continues to describe Artaud:

> His acting practice was based on the notion of exteriorization of an 'inner' truth: the physicalization of unconscious mental activity. And this is where the paradox is resolved: the outer truth, that is the motivation for behaviour, is translated into the codified corporeal narration that, by its very narration, provides for a material reality through which an inner truth can be revealed. And this, similar to the 'tai' and 'yu' of Japanese Noh, is a complete inversion of the Stanislavskian model.[13]

---

[13] Singleton, 'Artaud, East and West', in Schumacher and Singleton, eds, *Artaud on Theatre*, xxxiv.

This is not a question of subjectivity; it is the reverse, an expression of disinterest and detachment, an impersonal way of perceiving the present—one that is formed in a *kata*. Yachida-sama said: *Only to listen or hear is knowledge. When a person realizes something, he changes.*

Now, it seems to me that the act of reflecting is not the key to more profound understanding. In fact, reflection might be a way of distancing oneself from the event, and even of being shallow. Reflection is still as a mirror, engaging a conceptual plane that might not affect my body or my senses. By this, I remain in the realm of knowledge. The reflective act holds me back from the engagement of my sensible perception. If I only contemplate the idea of things, my senses cannot be affected; I need to get closer and be touched by a haptic surface, a texture, in order to let myself be moved by a consistency. This is what I think Gilles Deleuze means by 'being in the plane of immanence', the plane of consistency. To be touched is to *realize*, and that changes my way of acting. Spatial touching in this sense becomes emotional, and affective.

I become affected by my encounter with a certain spatiality. Instead of reflection, if I immerse myself into spatial awareness and open up for an unprejudiced meeting with potential perceptions, this might become a way of philosophizing with and through a concrete reality. The starting point is the concrete in which sensations becomes abstract through a pendulum movement between myopic and distanced receptive perception. Spatial encounters might develop a nonrepresentational and abstract particularized presence within my being.

Haecceity

Duns Scotus created the notion of haecceity in the middle ages, meaning 'this thing' or 'thisness'. Deleuze and Guattari introduce the word *haecceity* as a convergence of different modes:

> There is a mode of individuation very different from that of a person, subject, thing, or substance [...] A season, a winter, a summer, an hour, a date have a perfect individuality lacking nothing, even though this individuality is different from that of a thing or a subject. They are haecceities in the sense that they consist entirely of relations of movements and rest between molecules or particles, capacities to affect and be affected.[...], it also notes the importance of rain, hail, wind, [...]. Among types of civilizations, the Orient has many more individuations by haecceity than by subjectivity or substantiality: the haiku, for example, must include indicators as many floating lines constituting a complex individual.[14]

I recall my experience of the ecstasy of emptiness at Haguro Jinja. It was raining, drizzling on a diagonal. These were the elements: the direction of the pouring; the rhythm; the dim front drop; the tiny movements of drops that created a filter; a sonoric, visible and tactile veil.

---

14 Deleuze & Guattari, *A Thousand Plateaus* (London: Continuum, 2004), 287–88.

A haecceity has no beginning nor end, origin nor destination; it is always in the middle. It is not made of points, only of lines. It is a rhizome.[15]

Rhizomatic. No plot. No narration. The intensity is strong without a reason. No reason. No meaning. Just existing in the middle as a haecceity, a subtle spatial awareness. Where does an everyday act transgress suddenly into an existential, aesthetic emergence? This transgression may emerge gradually, but likewise can occur as an unexpected spontaneous haecceity. This reality has no structural narration; a surface intensity may consist of a dynamic concept without any narrative sense. At first sight, such a *trope* of the verbal description of the situation where I experienced the ecstasy of emptiness might actually appear naïve. But, as these words are placed upon a line—a temporal description of a multisensorial trope—this naïve situation as such is a complexity, is incommensurable, cannot be properly translated. Perhaps this notion of haecceity is closer to a description of the multisensible mode of existence. If so, haecceity is the format, and the taste or the character of a haecceity is that of an atmosphere. In this sense, *yūgen* is the taste or character of this haecceity.

Passage

Embodied emptiness to me is a feeling of a fuller emptiness, like a feeling of unborn relationships, a spatial awareness of potentiality. The Japanese notion of emptiness, *ku*, is not about a vacuum, for a vacuum is an empty emptiness. *Ku* means a possibility

15 Ibid., 290.

of giving space to intensity, a bodily hapticity that might emerge on the surface. We are now talking about spatial scales. Spatiality always relates to different scales. In the chapter 'Arguments from Inner Space', Brian Massumi stresses that we live between different dimensions:

> The body is composed of a branching network, decreasing in size right down to the level of molecular tubes at the mitochondrial scale. Geometrically, a body is a 'spacefilling fractal' of a 'fourth' dimensionality, between a two-dimensional plane and a three-dimensional volume.[16]

What Massumi argues is that skin is ostensibly a surface, but it is more than three-dimensional:

> Our skin obeys the laws of three dimensions [...] but our internal anatomy and physiology is living in a four-dimensional spatial world (the three of enveloping Euclidean space plus the 'fourth' fractal dimension of internal branching).[17]

This thinking leads to an understanding of the body not as 'a closed substance, but a passage, and the skin is a membrane with multiple openings that constitute a transformer in-between dif-

---

16 Brian Massumi, *Parables for the Virtual: Movement, Affect, Sensation* (Raleigh: Duke University Press, 2002), 202, citing Geoffrey B West, James H Brown, and Brian J Enquist, 'A General Model for the Origin of Allometric Scaling Laws in Biology', *Science* 276 (4 April 1997): 122–26. In all organisms 'essential materials are transported through space-filling fractal networks of branching tubes' (West, Brown, Enquist, 122).
17 Massumi's footnote: Geoffrey West, quoted in Roger Lewin, 'Ruling Passions', *New Scientist*, 3 April 1999, 39.

ferent dimensions'.[18] Massumi describes the body as a trope that forms a living act, an 'onto-topological', 'onto-genetic' act, and this is different from understanding the body and spatiality from the perspective of phenomenology. This is an existential trope, namely as Massumi says, *autopoietic*, an animating, moving emergence, which is not subjectivity, nor self. The *autopoietic* is a changing mode moved by necessity. Massumi emphasizes the impersonal aspect of this trope; it is in motion, involuntary and always becoming. The visibility and hapticity on the surface of things is nothing other than this relational effect of a hardening process, or a passage.

Morphology as Negative Gynaecology

The concept of *kata* indicates not only the effect as form, but the importance of the order of certain gestures to create form. In martial arts, *kata* implies the movements of the body not only as postures, but as the way to create these postures. In calligraphy this becomes very crucial. Each sign, or *kata*, has to be written with brushstrokes in a proper order. Yet despite such specificity, improvisation takes place. The discipline of *kata* is a critical preparation for independent improvisation to occur.

The concept of *kata* is difficult to understand outside its Japanese context. Maybe we have to understand the differentiation between Japanese aesthetics and modernism. One should be familiar with the importance of form in Japanese aesthetics. Form is distinguished from nothingness, emptiness, chaos, or disarray. Thus, in the world of dualism in which we live, form and non-form are re-

18 Massumi, *Parables for the Virtual*, 202.

lated to each other as two sides of the same coin. Non-form is as crucial as form. And non-form, or amorphology, is best expressed through the essence of each material in itself, as an *autopoiesis*. The essence is the highest level of a material's potential, and this expression is about the material's capacity to be in its highest potential. Such an invisible amorphous spatiality relates to a twin, its formalized form. This is the theory behind the Japanese concept of *iki* (simplicity, sophistication) a dual relationship to spatiality. In everyday life this could be expressed as female and male, and the tension in between these poles. In Japanese thinking, morphology is well expressed in terms of dualism: female and male *kata*.

This is remarkable when we look at the notion of morphology in the western tradition of aesthetics. Certain art forms do not exist as objects. In modernism, the dominant view of art is that it has a detached relationship to nature and its organic forms. This is an expression of dualistic differentiation; things (culture) have to distinguish themselves out from the background (nature). To see and value this relationship is a question of referring to something else. Things get their value in relation to their opposite. Art gets its (higher) value as something man-made in relation to nature, which is 'given'. Now, in the valuing process of cultural expressions, females suddenly get captured in a hidden trap. Those forms that are natural and refer to nature are not worth the same value as man-made forms. Distinguished art gets its value in relational opposition to the 'natural world' and its organic forms. Since the lawfulness of morphology occurs independently in nature, it is not highly ranked in the field of art, especially if it happens to be on a myopic scale.

Scale is an important feature in spatial awareness. From a western perspective, small scales in fine art tend to have less value, while large formats tend to be more important. So, what does a combination of a morphology of 'the amorphous' and small scale bring forth? Something highly valued in Japanese aesthetics. Amorphic forms have a very high value, and things on a small scale tend to have more precious value than those in colossal format.

German philosopher Peter Sloterdijk addresses these questions about morphology and proximity values as they relate to cultural expressions in his spherical philosophy as described in his book *Bubbles*.[19] His notion departs from an omitted peripheral phenomenon in western cultural history, namely *inner reality* and *proximity values* where things and spaces that are valued for their invisible way of touching us in our innermost consciousness, or because of an intimate spatial encounter. Sloterdijk stresses that even though the external realm and the world of objects have overtaken our culture, those sensible flows that strike and affect the innermost consciousness emerge from intimate atmospheres and attunements with other beings.

If we search back in time, we may find another history of morphology, what Sloterdijk calls 'nobjects', invisible to their form because they have no language. This can be seen the simple form of an egg. What takes place is not on the outside, but inside the confined space. He even coins a new trope, a 'negative gynaecology'[20]

---

19 Sloterdijk, *Spheres, Vol. 1: Bubbles Microspherology* (Los Angeles: Semiotexte, 2011).
20 See further in *Spheres*, chapter 4. 'The Retreat Within the Mother—Groundwork for a Negative Morphology', 269–291; and 'Excursus 2: Nobjects and Unrelationships—On the Revision of Psychoanalytical Stage Theory', 291–332.

which deals with a philosophical return to a feminine morphology and spatiality, an affirmation of the existential place and its forgotten forms: of wombs, hollows, and convexities. These are forms you cannot see from the outside. They are forms that are tactile and haptic from within, like the *Sazae* mollusc.

III

WE MIGHT THINK, from a visible stance, that the boundary between an invisible interiority and a visible exteriority is sharp where skin meets air. But is there really a division between these qualities? In my own work as an artist, I propose a grading scale of movement from a plane of consciousness to a physical body. In this way, the mental space emerges on the surface and becomes tactile, plastic and visible. A certain inner tension takes place in the air as in an aura where different kinds of subtle forces manifest into matter. The hapticity of the body is thus an extended consciousness. This is the meaning of the word incarnate (from Latin *carne*, 'flesh'), 'in a material body'. The body constitutes a channel, a passage between interior and exterior planes. What would happen if I add another layer, another skin to this channel and weave it between my body and the next spatiality? This is what I explore in my own artistic work. Spatiality is about a material relationship that takes place in the in-between-ness, in the emptiness. It is a concrete material link to the surrounding reality. I, too, am a material, and I relate to spatiality.

A holistic (nondualistic) awareness of topological textures that is both malleable and consistent is required to develop the skill for such sensible differentiation. The problem with dualistic perception is that touchable spatialities become a mere 'positive visuality', in other words, the visual part takes over the plane, and the invisible part is neglected. The neglected is the hidden side that exists as gaps and hollows and all non-formed amorphology that serve a relational role. With this holistic view, dualistic notions of beauty and ugliness are unnecessary. What concerns us is the awareness of a dynamic structural and spatial abstract perception seen from a non-representational perspective.

When I pay attention to something, I am not seeing representations as names and signs, but looking at the non-representation of phenomena by observing differentiation in itself, or the *nameless-ness* identity of things. What I see emerges from emptiness created by my prior non-awareness. In this way, emptiness is a concrete open space for emergences. These micro-acts of emergence are not decorative elements or curiosities; they are emergent atmospheric qualities that contain the richness of life, a fuller understanding of everyday spatiality.

These atmospheric qualities of *yūgen* form the *base note* in my own artistic work. I create atmospheres to emphasize unique moods that invite the viewer to act in a new way.

We are sensible subjects who perceive and are simultaneously the material of perception itself. In my art-making processes, I am concerned with how to become more attentive to subtle nuances, small scales, and ephemeral moments. If we are not attentive to these, we cannot value them, and they simply pass us by. Many of these sensibilities discussed here are not even occurrences in established fields of art. They emerge from real life, not from the realm of art. They emerge as intensities in the midst of a chaotic mingling of material, of high and low, ugly and beautiful things.

The physical appearance of our bodies is an ontological question. Nude or wrapped in a tissue, we are folds of *materia*. How are we enveloped? Coexistingly, I am layered in multiple textures. Smooth or striated, I dwell in hollows mingling with the world as a fluid materia. I am a part of spatiality as a volume, a density playing with light and shadow. This proximate scale of touching material, feeling surfaces, and smelling up close to the face, are aesthetico-existential acts, as Félix Guattari formulates. He sees a necessity for new aesthetic practices to develop a re-singularization as a way of starting from the subject without being driven by the mediated predefined subjectification process.

Ethico-Æsthetical Processuality

With *yūgen*, I encounter a vagueness that simultaneously concerns a distinct orientation; it grasps and seduces me, transforms me and changes me in constant movement. The artwork I created after returning from Sado Island is an investigation of spatial proximity values. This work, which I call a series of 'proposals', is first about making preparations for empty spaces where new kinds of participatory acts can take place that are proximate, immediate, and gentle—not monumental, detached, or conceptual. I have been seeking a sensory modality that might provide me with an alternative to the aesthetic paradigm, one where ethics are included in the experience of an ethico-aesthetical processuality. In these acts of becoming, the creative work is an ongoing process of revaluation, of self-cultivation.

Both in the West and in the East, ancient methods of self-cultivation were methods of shaping the self in relation to everyday life. Gesture, comportment, dress, habits, physical exercise, and diet all affected the potentiality of being a sensible, thinking subject. The Greek idea of self-cultivation described a way to refine, shape, and re-evaluate the ongoing processuality of becoming a concrete singularity. It was about the self-engaged with the common everyday as well as specific events.

In eastern culture, and specifically in Japanese aesthetics, more or less all art forms are practices of artistic self-cultivation. One can select different ways of self-cultivation in function with one's characteristics, inclinations and interests. The Way of Tea (*chado*), the Way of Swords (*kendo*), or the Way of Noh theatre, are all interrelated through the same thinking style: an ethico-aesthetic paradigm. These art forms address three dimensions: a mind and an alert spirit; a bodily-sensible awareness, comportment, and gesture; and a materiality, a surface of different scales. The aim of these arts is not to produce objects, but engage a processual self-cultivation of subtle refinement. These arts help bring about a revaluation of values regarding material and the world, such that the artist becomes a highly sensible singularity of reception and transmission. This requires a capacity to develop this differentiated consciousness—something that was valued in the pre-modern Japanese world as the highest social rank; in fact, the artist's taste stamped the hegemonic paradigm.[21]

---

21 Robert Carter, *The Japanese Arts and Self-Cultivation* (Albany: SUNY, 2008).

Conclusion

In my search for *yūgen*, I searched for philosophical notions, and I found these ethical-aesthetical ways of artistic self-cultivation. Is this anything new to me? It brings awareness to my habits. They domesticate me. I try to break these habits, and by doing this I rethink my own ways of working. Intuitive thinking is an immediate knowing. When followed by an act, it becomes a doing. This is the artist's way: to let oneself encounter all kinds of sensations, to be multisensorial. I collect sensations in my mind according to my inner references. Once stored, they might surface as emergences manifested as new occurrences. This process is so simple, yet the most incomprehensible to articulate as knowledge. This sensing is immediate experience that is here argued as knowledge. I need too many words to make it visible as an articulation, to turn the thinking into writing.

Today, words dominate our sensing of the world; many people think that non-articulated things don't even exist. But the verbal way is only one of many modes of articulation. The modern western world seems to have lost the ability to reconnect to other modes of sensing the world, modes which are the gateway to our senses. Our senses need to be used in a more receptive way to talk about what we perceive and to recognize perception as a non-verbal spatial attentiveness to a sensible world through a sensible body, mind, and consciousness.

But by doing that, perhaps I invite others into the artistic process of sensing and making. Sensing leads me to thinking; I continuously sketch the imaginary in my mind. The outlines emerge spontaneously as new thoughts, or become manifest as materiality in my actions. I continue to see my own articulations from a new perspective, as refreshed, rearticulated new cuts. This is life, this is art, silently emergences break into reality with immense force, with dynamic distinction. This expression of surfaces is not vague. If this irruption has an affect, it is seen as clear intensities upon the surface.

I think it is possible to find new ways to recreate ourselves and revalue the need for the sensible. Félix Guattari asks for a new ethico-aesthetic discipline:

> Rather than remaining subject, in periphery, to the seductive efficiency of economy competition, we must reappropriate Universes of value, so that processes of singularisation can rediscover their consistency. We need new social and aesthetic practices, new practices of the Self in relation to the other, to the foreign, the strange—a whole programme that seems far removed from current concerns.[22]

I am concerned with the necessity to relate to something more subtle, more proximate and myopic. To do this, I listen carefully to the senses through *receptive perception*, as the French philosopher Hélène Cixous expresses it. Closeness and subtle listening seem to go hand in hand with a slower tempo, but I think the problem is not the increased velocity. We cannot stop the world's flux; we have to move with it and instead let our thinking be volatile, like an attunement, but somehow still be on earth. In the chaotic everyday tempo, I strive to find the small threads that lead me to clearings. These clearings are concrete spatial spaces, myopic on my body, or

---

22 Félix Guattari, *The Three Ecologies* (London: Athlone Press, 2000), 45.

clearings in the urban forest, like cut-outs from the background or the foreground of an ongoing drama.

To describe this recognition of a new kind of perception, we might begin by asking a foundational question. What is the surface of things? It is a peel, like the last, ultimate layer of matter, a haptic visual of reality. This palpable layer is the place where acts emerge and become visible, creating an aesthetic. The etymology of the word 'aesthetic' derives from the Greek αἰσθητικός (*aisthētikos*), meaning 'from the senses'. We perceive through all our senses simultaneously; we live in a multisensible attunement. This reality is an ongoing real-time performance where our surroundings form our subject; we are moulded out of this reality like cut-outs from the background and foreground of the topology, 'the plane of consistency' as Deleuze puts it, literally and not as a metaphor.

The 'Place of Nothing' in Nishida as Chiasma and Chōra

JOHN W M KRUMMEL

¶ NISHIDA KITARŌ (西田幾多郎) (1870–1945), the founder of the twentieth century Japanese Kyoto School of philosophy, has been most noted for his philosophy of place (*basho* 場所) that he developed from 1926 until his death in 1945.[1] In order to articulate his novel notions, he made much use of nineteenth-century German philosophical terminology, especially the dialectical language of Hegel, and came to describe his own thinking as a kind dialectics. Such appropriations, especially of Hegelian terminology, however, seem inadequate in expressing what he strove to say— for his concept of *basho* confounds traditional western metaphysical discourse. The matter that he attempted to capture and express

---

1 This article is a modified version of chapter 10 of my book, *Place of Dialectic, Dialectic of Place: Nishida Kitarō and Chiasmatic Chorology* (Bloomington: Indiana University Press, 2015). All Japanese names in the present text will be indicated following the traditional Japanese convention with the family name first followed by the personal name. In this case, Nishida is the family name and his given name is Kitarō.

through the language of dialectics slips away from its structure, exploding beyond its bounds. The paper will explicate this *Sache* of Nishida's dialectic from the standpoint of his mature thought, especially from the 1930s and 40s. The two aspects of Nishida's thinking that I think confound traditional metaphysical discourse are what I call the *chiasmatic* aspect *of*, or implied *in*, his so-called 'dialectic' (*benshōhō* 弁証法) on the one hand, and the *chōra* that embraces or enfolds it, while expressing itself in it, on the other. *Chōra* enfolds and unfolds as *chiasma*. Combining these two terms I shall take the liberty of presenting Nishida's mature philosophy, what he calls his 'absolute dialectic' (*zettai benshōhō* 絶対弁証法) as a *chiasmatic chorology* in an attempt to better characterize the real matter of his thinking and to suggest that therein lies Nishida's own philosophical contribution that makes his work more than a mere appropriation or development of Hegelian dialectics or Mahāyāna non-dualism. I argue that it is due to its *chiasmatic* and *chōratic* nature that the *Sache* he strove to capture and express through the language of dialectical philosophy, perpetually slips away from any systemic bounds.

I will begin with a brief introduction to Nishida's philosophy of place before proceeding to show in what way Nishida's place is a *chiasma* and why it is a *chōra*. Viewing our embodied implacement in the world in terms of the *chiasmatic* and *chōratic* aspects of what Nishida means by *basho* would have significant implications for our contemporary situation in regard to globalization as well as to our relationship with nature. Hence I will end the discussion with some remarks on the relevance of this issue for us today.[2]

NISHIDA AND HIS THEORY OF PLACE

The first developed formulation of Nishida's concept of place (*basho*) appears in his essay 'Place' (*Basho*「場所」) that was first published in a journal *Tetsugaku kenkyū* (『哲学研究』) in 1926 and then inserted in his book *Hatarakumono kara mirumono e* (『働くものから見るものへ』; 'From the Working to the Seeing') in 1927. The purpose was to overcome the dichotomizing tendency so endemic to western philosophy and fully expressed in the epistemological dualism of the Neo-Kantians. The core issue for Nishida was the reference of the matter of cognition to something transcending its determination, the ground of its content that would establish objective knowledge, but which *in-itself* remains unknown (Z3 489).[3] How is that apparent gap between knower and known overcome (Z7 223), how does the structure of judgment relating the grammatical subject to its predicates correspond to the world? Nishida thus searched for a primitive unity that would ground the very possibility of knowledge. Rath-

---

[2] In writing this article, I was much inspired by the questions and suggestions received from participants at two different conferences where I presented its earlier incarnations: The International Conference on 'Japanese Philosophy as an Academic Discipline' held at the Chinese University of Hong Kong in December 2011, and the 7th Annual Meeting of the Comparative and Continental Philosophy Circle held in San Diegeo, California, March 2012.

[3] All references to Nishida's works in Japanese will be to the most recent editions of the collected works of Nishida: *Nishida Kitarō zenshū* (Tokyo: Iwanami, 2003). They will be indicated in the text in parentheses by Z followed by the volume number.

er than viewing the polarities—form and matter, subject and object—as separate entities, he grounded their unity with a focus on their holistic situation or context that encompasses and becomes differentiated, or 'formed', into them in the cognitive or judicative act (Z3 420, 481, 494, 496). He characterized this as a 'self-forming formlessness', a primitive undifferentiated unity, wherein ideal and real, experience and reality, are not yet separated out, the concrete situation lived prior to its bifurcation. Nishida initially formulated this idea in terms of a self-mirroring self-awareness but he needed a language that would vindicate him from the charge of psychologism and express the idea in logical rather than psychological terms. 'Place' (*basho*) was the term he found in order to express this dynamic holism.

This move to overcome dualism was also a move away from what he called 'object-logic' (*taishō ronri* 対象論理), the tendency in western thought to think in terms of objects, things that can be made into grammatical subjects of judgments. Nishida's reversal of object-logic was undertaken with a turn away from the grammatical subject in the direction of that which cannot be made into a subject of a statement, that which cannot be objectified. In a move to circumvent the habit of a substantializing or *thing*-centered view of reality, Nishida in his initial formulations thus identifies the predicate (*jutsugo* 述語) with *place* as what we ought to attend to. In other words, in opposition to the Aristotelian substance that 'becomes the grammatical subject but never a predicate', Nishida looks to *place* as the 'transcendent predicate' that determines the grammatical subject but itself remains un-objectifiable, incapable of being spoken of as a subject of judgment. In a subsumptive judgment, for example, it is the predicate *qua* universal wherein the grammatical subject as a particular may be said to be implaced. The universal as its determining predicate in this case is its *place* (see Z3 422, Z4 83). While universals may themselves be made into grammatical subjects of further judgments through subsumption into more encompassing universals, the ultimate universal would have to be no longer objectifiable, an unsayable indetermination that nevertheless must be assumed for determination. Nishida calls this most fundamental context behind every objectifying act, and necessarily presupposed, the place of true nothing (*shin no mu no basho* 真の無の場所) or the place of absolute nothing (*zettai mu no basho* 絶対無の場所). As the broadest and deepest background in its undifferentiated wholeness, it is 'absolutely nothing' to make possible the fore-ground emergence of beings *qua* objects. Nishida understands this to be the concrete contextual whole wherein we *always already* find ourselves implaced, and therefore necessarily presupposed by our cognitive or judicative acts. He was thus using the term 'predicate' as an heuristic device to turn our attention away from the object, the grammatical subject, to the contextual dimension or concrete field that environs what becomes the grammatical subject as well as the knower of that object, the one who makes the statement. In order to express this idea Nishida appropriates Hegel's notion of the concrete universal that determines itself through self-differentiation. The grammatical subject *qua* particular that is implaced in the universal is at the same time, in a reverse direction, an individuation through self-differentiation of that universal (see Z3 347–48, 390–91, 400, 402–3, 431, 464–65, 498, 517; Z4 81). In judgment, the grammatical subject is thus cut-out from its contextual matrix, which is therefore a 'place'.[4] For Nishida, however, that self-determining universal cannot be a concept or idea as it was for Hegel. He thought of it rather as the *pre*-conceptual *situation* of our concrete livedness, which he conceives in terms of an empty field wherein determination takes place and which he designates from 1926 on as 'place' (*basho*).

Nishida's initial formulation of the theory of place was the product of looking inward into the depths of self-awareness. In his later works, starting from the 1930s, however, Nishida turns his attention outward beyond the epistemological and psychological significances of place to speak of the contextual whole of the socio-historical world (*shakaiteki rekishiteki sekai* 社会的歴史的世界) that unfolds dialectically, and wherein the personal self interacts with others. This led him to develop the notion of a dialectical world (*benshōhōteki sekai* 弁証法的世界) wherein individuals in interaction and working upon the environment take part in the world's formation. Overcoming his former emphasis upon the predicate he thus comes to speak of the world (*sekai* 世界) as the medium for the mediation of universal and individual, predicate and subject. In what follows, I will base my reading of Nishida's

---

4 Nishida also refers to Hegel's etymological explanation of the German meaning of 'judgment' (*Urteil*) as a primordial differentiation or division (*ursprüngliche Teilung*) (Z3 331). See Hegel, *Encyclopedia Logic* in *Hegel's Logic*, §166, 231. Judgment is accordingly seen not as the combination of two independent terms—individual *qua* grammatical subject and universal *qua* predicate; or matter and form, determined and determining—but rather the self-differentiation of a concrete whole, its segmentation that makes explicit what is implied within it—the interrelation of its terms. For Hegel that differentiation in judgment is of the original concept (*Begriff*) of the whole. For Nishida however the whole is not a concept, it is pre-conceptual and something *lived*.

concept of place upon the standpoint of these later works of the 1930s and 40s.

DIALECTIC & CHIASMA

One of the central themes in Nishida's *benshōhō* (弁証法; 'dialectic') was the theme of contradictory self-identity (*mujunteki jikodōitsu* 矛盾的自己同一), an identity that by its very nature is not static but dynamic, involving the whole of oppositional processes. If dialectical logic involves the inter-relationship reflecting a system wherein the terms in relation are what they are only in their inter-relations and in the context set by their system, the dialectical whole,[5] Nishida's system may be included in the general category of what constitutes a 'dialectic'. Certainly, Nishida described his own depiction of reality as a 'dialectic'. The mature Nishida, in an attempt to preclude misunderstandings of his 'predicate logic', emphasizes that true self-identity, in its dialectical nature, can neither be objectified in the direction of what can be stated as a grammatical subject nor simply be conceived in the opposite direction of the thinking subjectivity *qua* absolute spirit or of absolutizing the predicate *qua* absolute concept. Rather he views his dialectic as involving genuine *inter*-determination that can never be reduced to either side of its terms. And this 'inter-determination' is what Nishida characterizes in terms of *mujun* (矛盾), 'contradiction' or 'paradox'.

---

5 See Joachim Israel, *The Language of Dialectic and the Dialectics of Language* (Atlantic Highlands, New Jersey: Humanities Press, 1979). And see G S Axtell's discussion of Israel's definition in his 'Comparative Dialectics: Nishida Kitaro's Logic of Place and Western Dialectical Thought', *Philosophy East and West*, 41.2 (April 1991): 176.

What does Nishida mean by 'contradiction' (*mujun*)? The term *mujun* comes from a Chinese story appearing in the text of *Han Feizi* (韓非子) wherein a vendor is selling lances (or halberds) and shields. On the one hand, the vendor advertises his lances as so sharp that there are no shields that the lances would fail to penetrate; but on the other he advertises his shields to be so strong and solid that nothing, no lances, can penetrate them. His characterizations are inconsistent; they are contradictory.[6] Nishida's dialectic involves the play between being and non-being, affirmation and negation, in other words, logical contradictories, which from a *trans*-logical perspective can be seen as bi-conditionals in that each implies the other and conditions the other as the contradictory that it is. Throughout the 1930s and 1940s, Nishida develops this into a *radical* dialectic involving mutual self-negation (*jiko hitei* 自己否定), precluding any conceptual synthetic resolution of the opposites.[7] The mediator is not a sublating concept but *mutual* self-negation, or from another perspective, their very field or *place* that is *nothing*. Any sort of self-affirmative act is seen to be predicated upon this prior self-negation: the self's affirmation requires its prior delimitation by environing conditions, a negation that can give shape to the affirmation. Its affirmation is obtained only in self-negation, i.e., de-substantialization, to preclude any substantial inter-obstruction of others. The self must come to terms with

6 The text in which the story appears was written during the end of the Warring States period (ca. 222 BCE) or the beginning of the Ch'in (Jp. Shin) Dynasty (221–206 BCE), the first unified state of China. See Han Fei Tzu, *The Complete Works of Han Fei Tzu*, trans. W K Liao (London: Arthur Probsthain, 1959), II, 143.
7 We should also keep in mind here that 'radical' comes from the Latin root *radix*, which refers to 'the root of things'.

its fact of finitude or contingency in a self-negation *vis-à-vis* the world acting upon it. And such self-negation, on the part of each individual, mirrors the absolute nothing (*zettai mu* 絶対無) that is the place of the world's dialectical self-formations (*via* self-negations). It mirrors the self-negation of an abysmal place that *qua* world clears room for the emergence of correlative beings (see Z10 315–16). The relationship between the individual and the world involves this radical interdependence *via* mutual self-negation. The entire world is a unity-in-flux of such contradictories, irreducible to any simple identity.

Nishida is also careful to avoid any sort of nihilism that might result from self-negation and that would deny the reality of the world of things. Self-negation is a double negation that is not a mere negation *vis-à-vis* the positive. Absolute nothing encompasses both negativity and positivity, non-being and being, destruction and creation, as a 'middle' irreducible to either terms. The place of the world escapes *both* reification as substance *and* annihilation into utter nothing. Insofar as its self-negation is what makes room for beings, creating and affirming them, it is positive. It is a fecund nothing, an undefinable potential that unfolds in its actualizations. Nishida's dialectic thus involves logical contradiction but it is seen from a broader perspectival stance that witnesses the very relationship of contradiction. That is, it encompasses logical contradiction but for that reason refuses reduction to the mere terms of being or non-being, *on* or *mēon*, affirmation or negation, positivity or negativity.

Broader and deeper than what can be reduced to the dialectical structure of bi-conditional opposites, Nishida's absolute dialectic—with its multi-dimensional complexity of a self-determining matrix—involves a *chiasma* of (over)inter-determinations. By *chiasma* I mean the radical multi-dimensional relationality of reality that Nishida recognizes. Does this *chiasma* undermine the very language of that 'dialectic'? *Chiasma* is a term used in anatomy and in genetics, and in general refers to a 'crossing'. The word comes from the Greek *chiasma* (χίασμα), meaning 'cross-piece', 'crossover', or 'x-shape'. It also comes from the Greek *chiazein*, meaning 'to mark with an x', and the Greek letter *chi* (X, χ). I use *chiasma* and *chiasmatic* here to refer to the cross-configuration or intersection between the horizontal inter-relationality amongst individuals (relative beings) and the vertical inter-relationality between individuals and what envelops and embraces them—understood in the various terms of place, world, absolute, nothing, etc.—in Nishida. This means also, for example, the various cross-dimensional intersections between the spatial and the temporal, vertical and horizontal, linear and circular, individual and universal, the body and its social and natural environments, etc., that we find in Nishida's thinking. By taking Nishida's 'contradiction' (*mujun*) as a *chiasma*, we can focus upon its character as an inter-dimensional cross-section where opposites, *including contradictories*, meet and condition each other, and as the source from out of which they are abstracted. The expression of contradictory self-identity seems to depict, however, only the tip of the iceberg of a vast complexity that is *chiasmatic*. While Nishida at times emphasizes *logical* contradiction in its ontological significance, i.e., yes and no as being and non-being—so that even time and space become viewed in their mutual exclusivity, i.e., time is *not* space and space is *not* time—we might also take this as a surface manifestation or expression of a logically irreducible plethora[8] of a manifold in *chiasmatic* interaction.

Chiasma is not exactly the same in significance as *chiasmus*. The dictionary distinguishes these two related words. The latter is a figure of speech based on an inverted parallelism, whereby the order of terms in parallel clauses is reversed in one of the clauses (e.g., 'one should eat to live, not live to eat'.) This sense seems to approach what Maurice Merleau-Ponty tries to capture with his notion of *chiasm*, which might be defined as the paradoxical form of a whole composed of parts interrelating in inverse structural orders.[9] I take *chiasma*, however, to be inclusive of the meanings of *chiasmus* and the Merleau-Pontyan *chiasm* in that the multi-layered criss-crossing would also involve a kind of reciprocity and multiple inversions, albeit with certain irreversible disjunctions between the terms. One notices this, for example, in Nishida's notions of the dialectical interdetermination between individual and environment,

---

8 This means that even the basic contradiction between life or birth and death might be viewed as inseparable intertwining bi-conditionals within a complex *chiasma* of multiple processes on a variety of levels, e.g., social-ethical, physical, biological, etc. Here I do not intend to dismiss the existential significance in Nishida of one's encounter with death in its alterity and negation of the self. The plurality into which one disperses in death and out of which the unity of the self is born in itself can be viewed as the *otherness* of the not-self.

9 An example, suggested by Andrew Feenberg in his discussion of this would be history as what is 'drawn' by the subject and what 'draws' the subject. See Maurice Merleau-Ponty, *The Visible and the Invisible* (Evanston, Illinois: Northwestern University Press, 1968), 130ff, especially 138; Yoko Arisaka and Andrew Feenberg, 'Experiential Ontology: The Origins of the Nishida Philosophy in the Doctrine of Pure Experience', *International Philosophical Quarterly* 30.2 (June 1990): 202; and Andrew Feenberg, 'Experience and Culture: Nishida's Path "To the Things Themselves"', *Philosophy East and West* 49.1 (1999): 38. For some more discussions bringing Merleau-Ponty and Nishida into dialogue, see the essays in Jin Y Park and Gereon Kopf, eds., *Merleau-Ponty and Buddhism* (Lanham, Kentucky: Lexington Books, 2009).

of the universal's determination of the individual and its reverse determination (*gyaku gentei* 逆限定) by the individual, and of the inverse correspondence (*gyakutaiō* 逆対応) between absolute and finite, as we shall see further below.

Even in his earlier works, such as in *Geijutsu to dōtoku* (『芸術と道徳』; *Art and Morality*) of 1923, Nishida had already recognized the *chiasmatic* nature of the concrete in terms of our embodiment that connects our subjectivity with objects, while also serving as the locus for the inter-section (*kōsa* 交差) between the object-world of cognition and the object-world of volition. The body with its sensibility and motility serves to connect the various object-worlds of facts, truth, reality, beauty, and good, whereby we can enter into and exit each world (Z3 246). And a little later in *Hyōgen sayō* (「表現作用」; *Act of Expression*) of 1925, Nishida speaks of the 'cross-section' (*kōsaten* 交差点) between the ideal and the real in the body where content, expression, and act all intersect. And the world is also such a cross-section between volition and cognition (Z3 382). The significance of the body in the 1930s deepens that *chiasmatic* aspect as an intersection that gathers various forces into a microcosmic creative funnel whereby the world creates itself in our 'acting-intuitions'.[10] The human body it-

---

10 Acting-intuition (*kōiteki chokkan* 行為的直観) describes the dialectic of seeing things by working upon them in inter-activity with the world. To understand things already implies our acting upon them, giving them form within the context of the given historical world. In turn our awareness is shaped as we interactively work upon the environment. The dialectic is such that we are both passively determined by the environment and actively working upon it. The two moments of acting and seeing, activity and passivity, cannot be divorced. And acting-intuition as such occurs in pre-judicative, pre-theoretical, immediacy with the world.

self thus serves, in its very inter-activity, as a place of intersection, a *chiasma*. While musing upon this *chiasmatic* nature of the body, Nishida also develops the *chiasma* on a macrocosmic level, taking the creative world to be a world of inter-action (*aihataraki* 相働き) between individuals that are simultaneously active and passive, affirmative and negative, toward each other. Their bodies are thus influenced by others as something made (*tsukurareta mono* 作られたもの) but simultaneously influence others as something creative (*tsukuru mono* 作るもの) (see Z8 299/LL 27–28; Z10 94, 97–98). Embodiment is at the criss-crossing intersection of the world where the horizontal (interaction with other bodies) and the vertical (interaction with the world as a whole) meet, as a *chiasmatic* axis uniting inner and outer, self and environment, individual and universal, affirmation and negation, subjective and objective, time and space, etc.

In this respect, in discussing the *chiasma* in Nishida, the significance of the body (*shintai* 身体) in its interrelationality with the world cannot be ignored. This *chiasma* becomes evident through man's embodied interrelations with the environment, wherein production or creation is the exemplary mode. Human beings alter the environment by making things. In turn, human beings are made by what they make. We act upon some material to give it form, but in turn are acted upon by the product. We ourselves are made in the very process of making. Our body is hence formed and forming, *creata et creans* (Z8 32; Z10 114). And this also means for Nishida that the world is making us as we participate in its creative dynamism. We are operative and formative elements *within* the creative world (*sōzōteki sekai* 創造的世界) (Z8 64). As such we are both the subjects and the objects of the world's formation. And this bodily interactivity extends its significance to encompass the technological alteration of the world as we employ our bodies as means for making and handling tools in the world's formation (see Z8 14, 22, 50, 63, 67). In this process tools become incorporated into the body and become its extension. We might think of examples, such as the blind man's cane, a skillful driver's car, the painter's brush, or a sculptor's chiseling and carving tools. And even the world as means to our ends, and thus as a 'tool', becomes an extension of our body (see Z8 45). The body in this sense as living or lived (as *Leib*) thus extends beyond its merely corporeal limits (as *Körper*). Such *chiasmatic* interworking, whereby the eco-environment becomes the mediating body, extending our being into nature, rejects any nature-culture dichotomy. The situation underscores ambiguity of the body as neither mere tool (as object) nor merely its user (as subject) (See Z8 32, 46). There is then no static demarcation between self as embodied and its surroundings. But this also means that, like the human body, the environing world as well is ambiguous as forming and formed. In Nishidian terms, both are 'self-contradictory' (*jikomujunteki* 自己矛盾的). For the world is both the *place* and *product* of its movements. While we form it, we are also implaced within it to be determined by it. Our body is the *chiasmatic* medium of our forming and being-formed *vis-à-vis* the world as well as the *chiasmatic* focal point for the world's self-formations. It is a *chiasmatic* vector of the cosmic *chiasma* as the world of interactivity. In that sense we might even speak of a *genesis* of reality in the growing-together of environment and body through their *chiasmatic* interactions that give form to place.

Nishida characterizes the dialectical structure of the world as a whole, *the dialectical universal* (*benshōhōteki ippansha* 弁証法的一般者). In its manifold dialectic expressed in the world's formation, what on the vertical plane is the universal's self-determination and its reverse determination by the individual, on the horizontal plane is the inter-determinations of individuals belonging to that universal. The *chiasmatic* inter-reactions between them on these different planes constitute the unfolding of the world-matrix in society and history. The vertical and the horizontal here are inseparable in that they are different ways of speaking of the same dialectical matrix: the universal's self-determination *is* the individuals' co-determinations, and neither side can be prioritized over the other or reduced to the other. The different directions and planes of dialectical determination are mutually implicative so that the dialectical universal's self-determination means the individual's self-determination, and the individual's self-determination also implies inter-determination among individuals, which in turn also means the self-determination of the universal to constitute the world of those individuals (see Z6 236–37). Hence, as Nishida states, the world is thoroughly universal and thoroughly of individuals (Z6 159). The matrix simultaneously is *both* universal determination *and* individual determination (Z6 234). We can comprehend that reciprocity involving the self-determination of the universal and the mutual determinations of individual beings conjoined *via* contradictory identity and inverse correspondence, as an inter-dimensional and inter-directional *chiasma*. Universal and individual meet in the *chiasma* of inter-determinations. Moreover the *chiasma* in its radical reciprocity—in its reverse determinations, mutual self-negations, and inverse correspondences—involves a *chiasmus* that must extend in complexity beyond triadic formulas of bi-nomial interplay. What we have here is a *chiasmatic* inter-crossing of dimensions. With its maturation in the 1930s, Nishida's dialectic between subjectivity and objectivity, inner and outer, thus comes to involve the interrelationship between the world as whole and the individual person as the world's elemental part, and between the individual's internal self-determination that Nishida metaphorically characterizes as 'linear' in time and the world's external determination metaphorically characterized as 'circular' in space. The co-determinations of these various dimensions, whereby 'inner is outer and outer is inner', meet in the *chiasma* of the world-matrix that is neither simply ideal nor merely material.

Nishida characterizes that world-matrix in terms of Pascal's (and Nicholas of Cusa's) infinite sphere without periphery with everywhere its center.[11] We would have to conceive this spherical unlimitedness as being filled *chiasmatically* with such criss-crossing intersections even while substantially being 'nothing'. The world of matter and the world of consciousness ultimately are what be-

---

11 See Blaise Pascal, *Pensées*, trans. A J Krailsheimer (London: Penguin, 1995, 1966), sec. 199 (§72), 60. Prior to Pascal this idea was expressed by Nicholas of Cusa. See Nicholas of Cusa, *De docta ingorantia* ('On Learned Ignorance') in *Nicholas of Cusa: Selected Spiritual Writings*, trans. H Lawrence Bond (New York: Paulist Press, 1997), 116ff. Nicholas' claim here that the universe's circumference is nowhere and its center everywhere is in its turn derived from a twelfth-century pseudo-Hermetic text, 'The Book of the XXIV Philosophers'. Later in the sixteenth century Giordano Bruno and then in the seventeenth century Pascal borrow this idea. But none of these writers cite the original source from which they took this idea. Edward Casey discusses this in his *Fate of Place: A Philosophical History* (Berkeley: University of California Press, 1997), 116–117, 385, notes 43–44.

come abstracted out of that *chiasmatic* sphere as their concrete but empty foundation. And in turn the embodied individual mirrors that macrocosmic *chiasma* as a *chiasmatic* microcosm, the meeting point of the diverse dimensions, caught in-between the 'two abysses of the infinite whole and of nothing'.[12]

This *chiasmatic* sphere certainly has spatial significance but that 'spatiality' also encompasses time. For Nishida understands the 'eternal present' (*eien no genzai* 永遠の現在) as a place that enfolds and unfolds time.[13] Concrete reality is realized in that surface point of the present, concentrating an unfathomable *chiasmatic* complexity where temporal and spatial axes intercept. But the present as 'a place of nothing' is abysmal in nature, an abyss that serves to be the source of novelty as well as of freedom and creativity. The determinist hold of mechanistic causality is thereby loosened. Human creativity as partaking in world formation would be predicated upon the seizure, in self-awareness, of the singularity of the here-and-now *vis-à-vis* that abyss, realizing the inter-section, the *chiasma*, of spatial and temporal conditions. In his reading of Nishida, Nakamura Yūjirō[14] relegates the horizontal dimension of this dialectic to the moment-to-moment temporalizing sequence of its process unfolding in time. However since

12 Pascal, *Pensées*, sec. 199 (§72), 61.
13 We might add here that Nishida's concept of depth in the ordinary (*byōjōtei* 平常底) from the 1940s also exemplifies this cross-sectional *chiasma* of temporal and spatial interrelations, horizontal and vertical interrelations, whereby depth is manifest at the very surface.
14 See Nakamura Yūjiō, *Nishida Kitarō* (Tokyo: Midorigawa, 1983) and Nakamura Yūjirō, *Nishida Kitarō no datsukōchiku* [*The Deconstruction of Nishida Kitaro*] (Tokyo: Iwanami, 1987). The former was republished as *Nishida Kitarō I* (Tokyo: Iwanami, 2001) and the latter was republished as *Nishida Kitarō II* (Tokyo: Iwanami, 2001).

inter-determination also occurs among the spatially co-relative, we ought to recognize the spatiality of the horizontal *as well*, allowing for the synchrony of co-determination among events or individuals. The horizontal cannot be restricted to time because interrelations among co-relative beings happen not only diachronically but also synchronically. As Nishida himself states in *Tetsugaku no konpon mondai* (『哲学の根本問題』; *Fundamental Problems of Philosophy*) the mutual determination of individuals cannot be understood in light of mere process (Z6 74).[15] Furthermore, along with temporality and spatiality, what Nishida means by *place* must encompass the spatiality of *both* the vertical and the horizontal dimensions. The *chiasmatic* nature of the world-matrix as *place* then would be *both* horizontal as the spatial field of co-relative beings and the temporal course of successive beings; *and* vertical in its own self-negating inversion that makes room not only for those horizontal relations but also for its relationship *qua* place with the implaced—or: *qua* absolute with the relative, or *qua* nothing with beings. While the vertical in the self-emptying process—what Nishida comes to call inverse correspondence—collapses into the horizontal in the interrelations among beings, it simultaneously encompasses the horizontal in giving it space. It is the incalculable

15 The original reads: '...tann naru kateiteki benshōhō kara kobutsu to kobutsu to no sōgōkankei to iūmono wa kangaerarenai' (Z6 74). Dilworth translates this as: '...mutual determination of individuals is not merely a dialectical process' (*Fundamental Problems of Philosophy: The World of Action and the Dialectical World*, trans. David Dilworth [Tokyo: Sophia University, 1970], 47). However *kateiteki benshōhō* has the sense of 'dialectic of process' rather than simply 'dialectical process'. That is, it has the significance of a certain type of dialectic, namely the dialectic of process, as opposed to another type of dialectic, namely Nishida's own dialectic of *basho*, that takes 'spatial' or synchronic relations into consideration.

complexity in the compounding of these many dimensions—horizontal and vertical, synchrony and diachrony—grounded upon an un/grounding abyss, that accounts for unpredictability and indeterminacy in the history of the world (see illustration 1).[16] So the 'spatiality' of the infinite sphere here is really *trans*-spatial. It encompasses the horizonality of *both* space and time as media for the interrelations and inter-determinations between individual actors and between individual moments. *And* it also encompasses the sphere's own vertical interrelations and inter-determinations with those individual elements (in space-time). The matrix of the world, the concrete place of reality, is an infinite self-inverting space-time *chiasma*, an indefinite openness that in itself is both *trans*-temporal and *trans*-spatial. *Basho* or place, we might say, is this cross-dimensional self-inverting *chiasmatic* spatiality of the world. But paradoxically, in making-room even for its own self-negation that in turn makes-room for beings—making space for its making space for beings—this space is a space that escapes geometrical representation. As I stated above, it is a trans-temporal and trans-spatial space.

In the late 1930s Nishida also names that structuring of the concrete, *logos*. It is the structuring of reality wherein there is inter-resonance *via* mutual self-negation and contradictory self-identity between universal and individual, whole and part, world and element. Nishida's *logos* then involves the *chiasmatic* structuring of multi-levels, dimensions, and directions; it really names what *exceeds* the logical. The world *qua* dialectical universal is a multi-

---

16 This figure was originally created for and first appears in my article, 'Embodied Implacement in Kūkai and Nishida', *Philosophy East and West* 65.3 (July 2015).

directional *chiasma* of inter-dimensional self-negation. First and foremost, prior to any theoretical abstractions or reductions, we find ourselves implaced within this concrete *chiasma*, wherein we are born, dwell, and die, and wherein we are generated and perish at every moment upon an abyss (see Z8 38). We take part in that *chiasmatic legein*, or 'gathering', of *logos*. And thus we can also speak of the *chiasma* in one's own deep personal and existential dimension—the *chiasma* in the depths of one's being, where one crosses the threshold between life and death, being and nothing, wherein one directly confronts one's contradictory identity and one's inverse correspondence with the absolute place of one's implacement, the dimension of what Nishida calls 'the religious' (*shūkyōteki* 宗教的) where we come face-to-face with alterity defining our finitude.

The *chiasma* of inter-dimensional inter-determinations—vertically and horizontally, in 'linear' time and in 'circular' space, microcosmically and macrocosmically—is the world's matrix, the *logos* of its unfolding. But this matrix, whose elements are mediated by self-negation, is itself non-substantial. For its radically *chiasmatic* nature precludes the very possibility of substantialization. To construe Nishida's philosophy as comparable to Spinozism and as promoting a 'one body that is non-dual' (*ittai funi* 一体不二), even if both Nishida and Spinoza look to a 'universal principle as God', is then highly dubious.[17] Kosaka Kunitsugu's emphasis of the non-discrimination and equality between self and

---

17 See Kosaka Kunitsugu, *Nishida Kitarō o meguru tetsugakusha gunzō* (Kyoto: Mineruva shobō, 1997), chapters 3–5; and see Gereon Kopf's critique of it in 'On the Brink of Postmodernity: Recent Japanese-Language Publications on the Philosophy of Nishida Kitarō', *Japanese Journal of Religious Studies* 30.1–2 (2003): 138.

CHIASMA AND CHŌRA

ILLUSTRATION 1.
THE DIALECTIC OF PLACE AS A DIALECTIC OF
VERTICAL AND HORIZONTAL INTER-DETERMINATION.

Zettai mu 絶対無 [*absolute nothing*] *as an undetermined basho* 場所 [*place*] *that self-negates to make room for beings.*

Vertical Line: gyakutaiô 逆対応 [*inverse polarity/correspondence*] *and zettai mujunteki jikodôitsu* 絶対矛盾的自己同一 [*absolutely contradictory self-identity*];

mutual self-negation between nothing and beings, absolute and co-relatives, one and many, place and implaced.

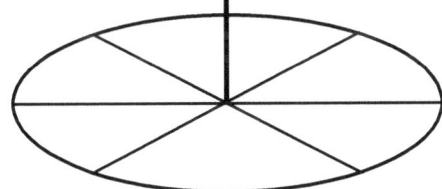

Horizontal plane: co-relativity of beings. This plane is both temporal and spatial since the interdependence amongst thing-events entails both diachronic and synchronic relationships.

Zettai mu 絶対無 [absolute nothing] as an undetermined basho 場所 [place] that self-negates to make room for beings. The place of absolute nothing [zettaimu no basho 絶対無の場所] is non-distinct from the place of beings [yû no basho 有の場所] and not transcendent to it. Beings are interdependent both diachronically and synchronically, thus temporally and spatially. When seen vis-à-vis absolutely nothing (as delimited by it or as its self-determination), this place is a circle, or rather a sphere, without periphery or center. Acting-intuition [kôiteki chokkan 行為的直観] of the historical body [rekishiteki shintai 歴史的身体] dialectically moves "from the made/created to the making/creating," expressing the horizontal interrelationship between individual self and environment of other individual things and persons, but also expressing the vertical interrelationship between the self-forming world and individuals as its formative elements.

world, individual and universal, and the utter elimination of any distinction between subjectivity and objectivity, inner and outer, one and many, absolute and relative, etc., accomplished *via* an exhaustive self-negation, is somewhat misleading.[18] This still sounds like a kind of monism whereby everything sinks into nothingness. It downplays the very tension between these opposites that are never resolved whether under an absolute concept or an absolute substance or even under utter nothingness. Nishida himself distinguishes his thinking from Spinoza's. The difference is obvious when we notice that Nishida's universal is not a substance and escapes being made into a grammatical subject of a sentence. The *chiasmatic* nature of his dynamic non-dualism precludes any universalizing monism as well as any self-affirmation, from the other end, regarding the ultimacy of the individual *qua* substance. As Ueda Shizuteru states, neither the one nor the many, neither monism nor dualism nor pluralism is taken as the foundation.[19] Concrete reality is non-substantial because it is predicated upon difference, alterity, and inter-relationality. Substance emerges only in abstraction from that concreteness. The path that Nishida treads thus avoids the pitfalls of an absolutizing conceptualism or substantialism on the one hand, as well as nihilism on the other. Nishida's stance is rather one of what Ueda calls a 'dynamic non-foundationalist multi-dimensionalism'.[20] Its dynamic tension—the *chiasma*—is the 'Dionysian dance from out of which gods are born' (Z8 396–97).[21]

18 Kosaka Kunitsugu, *Nishida Kitarō no shisō* (Tokyo: Kōdansha, 2002), 301–2.
19 Shizuteru Ueda, 'Pure Experience, Self-Awareness, Basho', *Études phénoménologiques* 18 (1993): 67.
20 Ibid.
21 Nishida here is referring to an idea found in Jane Ellen Harrison's *Themis: A Study of the Social Origins of Greek Religion* (Cambridge: Cambridge University Press, 1912), 13–14.

Hence we might say that Nishida's philosophy, in its 'logic of contradictory self-identity'—the dialectic of the dialectical universal that is really a dialectic of negation—implies, as opposed to Aristotelian *ousiology*—a 'logic of substance', i.e., a logic of non-contradictory identity—a *chiasmology*. Perhaps the language of the 'logic of contradiction' can then be re-stated in terms of a field of an inter-acting or inter-folding mani-fold, a *chiasmology*, the *legein* of *chiasma*. As mentioned briefly above, if 'dialectic' is but the interrelationship between two opposites, even as bi-conditionals, it would seem to be a simplification of, or abstraction from, what concretely speaking is a *chiasma* of multiple disparates, or of an inter-folding mani-fold of an abysmal *place* constituting identities through mutual differences in those folds. Taking our discussion beyond Nishidian formulations, the dialectic of bi-conditional opposites or contradictories then ultimately gives way to a *chiasma* of manifold forces and dimensions in (over)inter-determination, each term of which precludes reduction to any other in virtue of its own *chiasmatic* complexity. The criss-crossing of multiple factors on multi-dimensional levels exceed in complexity binomial oppositions or even the triadic formula of traditional dialectic. The complexity is one of over-determination that threatens to undermine the very language of traditional dialectics. Even the primal opposition between being and non-being would have to dissolve into this *chiasma* of manifold *chiasmas*, each of which is too complex to be declared merely 'being' or 'non-being', 'is' or 'is-not'. It is not that there are two distinct absolute principles that we name 'being' and 'non-being', which subsequently oppose and inter-relate to constitute things; rather the very enfolding-unfolding play of being and non-being that constitute the finitude of things itself consists of a *chiasmatic* manifold of forces or folds, each in turn irreducibly composed of further such *chiasmas*. The *chiasmatic* manifold of *chiasmas*, extending without end outwardly and inwardly, to explode and implode de-limiting boundaries, is thus what would constitute the infinite sphere without periphery. The *chiasma* as such deconstructs any notion of a substance. The Greek term for Aristotle's substance, *ousia* (οὐσία), is also the abstract noun form for the verb *einai* (εἶναι), 'to be'. In contrast to the Aristotelian *ousiology* of being, the *chiasmology* points to a cross-sectional place of manifold intricate inter-activities. This is what surfaces in Nishida's terms of the contradictory identity between *on* (ον, 'being') and *mēon* (μηον, 'non-being'). If Aristotle's *ousiology* is an *ontology*, Nishida's *chiasmology* is then an *an-ontology*, implying the en-folding intertwining of *on* and *mēon* within a *chiasmatic* manifold.[22] That place of *chiasma*, enveloping the manifold, is what Nishida calls *basho*. The *chiasma* (over)determines that otherwise indeterminate place of nothing. To that *place* in its self-withdrawing, self-negating character, making possible the *chiasmatic* (over) inter-determinations, we now turn.

PLACE & CHŌRA

Nishida's claim in regard to place was that everything is in a place, every place is in *its* place, and ultimately everything and every

---

22 I neologize the term *anontology* to characterize this structure of *basho* as what Nishida calls *absolute* negation. We cannot call it *meontology* because μη (*mē*) is still a conditional adverb (e.g., 'I think not...'). I use *anontology*, on the other hand, to mean the structure encompassing both *on* and *mēon*, or being and non-being, ultimately referring to the place of absolute nothing.

place is encompassed by *nothing*: the place of absolute nothing (*zettai mu no basho*). In the beginning of his 1926 essay, '*Basho*' ('Place'), Nishida tells us that he drew inspiration for this idea from Plato's concept of *chōra* (χώρα) in the *Timaeus* and adapted it to his concerns. In the *Timaeus* (52B), for example, it is said: 'everything that exists must of necessity be somewhere, in some place [*topos*, τόπος] and occupying some *chōra*, and that that which doesn't exist somewhere, whether on earth or in the heavens, doesn't exist at all'.[23] It may help us to understand Nishida's dialectic of place if we examine the implications of this Greek notion.

In the initial stages of his *basho*-theory, where his concern was primarily to overcome epistemological dualism, Nishida adapts Plato's *chōra* to that epistemological subject-object sphere. Thereby he transposes the Platonic *ideas* into epistemological categories that form sense-matter, and *chōra* becomes the place *qua* field of consciousness (*ishiki no ba* 意識の場) for that interrelationship of form and matter (see Z3 415, 498; Z10 59). But the final place that is delimited by nothing would have to envelop both subjectivity and objectivity, *noesis* and *noema*. Thus, while taking over the Neo-Kantian appropriation of Platonist thought, Nishida regarded the field of consciousness as a place of *relative* or *oppositional* nothing (*sōtai mu* 相対無, *tairitsuteki mu no basho* 対立的無の場所) in relation to its objects that are thus beings (*yū* 有).

Ueda Shizuteru understands Nishida's *basho* to involve a multi-layered structuring of meanings, a horizon of meaning for experience that constitutes the place wherein one *always already* finds

---

23 Plato's *Timaeus* in *Complete Works*, ed. John M Cooper (Indianapolis: Hackett, 1997), 1255. The translation is by Donald J Zeyl.

oneself existing. Each horizon of experience is in itself always limited, implying a 'beyond' that constitutes the very condition for the horizon's possibility.[24] That 'beyond' is always dark and unknowable, unobjectifiable, what Nishida called *mu* (無; nothing). And yet to acknowledge it is 'self-awareness' or 'self-realizing' (*jikaku* 自覚). A significant point here is that in his very attempt to construct a complete system of self-awareness that would surmount the gap of Kantian dualism, Nishida has ingeniously allowed for the very impossibility of its completion as an aspect integral to his 'complete' account.[25] Yoko Arisaka has thus pointed out that Nishida's theory is an attempt to construct a theoretical system that is in

24 Ueda, 'Pure Experience', 80.
25 On this and the following, see Yoko Arisaka, 'System and Existence: Nishida's Logic of Place' in Augustin Berque, ed., *Logique du lieu et dépassement de la modernité* (Brussels: Ousia, 1999), 44.

herently irreducible to thought by virtue of its unreifiable concrete source, a self-grounding principle of un-groundedness, the nothing that horizons as an open system, a 'circle without periphery'. What Nishida comes to call 'the world' (sekai) in the 1930s can then be viewed in light of that final *place* or horizon of sense (meaning) encompassing the other delimited places. On the other hand, if we take the 'world' itself as a delimited and restricted horizon, it would imply yet a further openness enveloping it, itself unrestricted, undelimited, the open that Nishida calls the place of absolute nothing, which in the world-dialectic of the 1930s comes to take on the significance of that *trans-temporal* and *trans-spatial* space, enfolding and unfolding its *chiasmology* as we discussed above. Our being-in-the-world essentially involves our implacement within the world, in turn, implaced within that open sphere without periphery.[26] And the self-determining open sphere that is the world's matrix is the field, *place*, of the inter-dimensional, inter-directional, inter-determining *chiasma* that we touched upon above. It is this *open* however that we may further understand in terms of *chōra* in its more than merely epistemological significance.

Why *chōra*? The Greek term has been variously translated as 'place', 'space', 'country', 'region', 'land', 'area'. In ordinary non-philosophical and pre-Platonic Greek it connotes the 'country' opposing or surrounding the city or town. In Plato's *Timaeus*, the term is used to mean the 'receptacle' (*hupodochē*) onto which the *ideas* are in-formed or in-scribed to make their particular copies that occupy and give shape to the *cosmos* or 'world'. The character Timaeus, after whom the book is named, explains:

> Not only does it always receive all things, it has never in any way whatever taken on any form [*morphē*] like any of those things that enter it. For its nature is to be a matrix [*ekmageion*] for all things; and it is modified, shaped, and reshaped by those things that enter it. These are the things that make it appear different at different times. (50B–C)[27]

This idea of *chōra* expresses an in-definition that is neither subjective nor objective, neither *idea* nor thing, neither paradigm nor copy. It is the third 'something' or genus—*triton genos* (52A)—ne-

26 On the world's implacement in an 'unrestricted openness', see Ueda, 'Pure Experience', 78–79.
27 Plato, *Complete Works*, 1253. The translation here is slightly modified on the basis of Edward S Casey, 'Smooth Spaces and Rough-edged Places: The Hidden History of Place', *The Review of Metaphysics* 51 (December 1997): 271; and John Sallis, *Chorology: On Beginning in Plato's Timaeus* (Bloomington: Indiana University Press, 1999), 108.

cessitated by the relationship between copy (thing) and paradigm (*idea*), i.e., between the formed individual *qua* 'becoming' (*genesis*) and the forming universal *idea qua* 'being' (*on*), for 'the image must be *in* something and made *out of* something other than that of which it is an image'.[28] Because it *receives* the *types* (*ideas*) and gives them *place*, Timaeus names that *something* 'place' (*chōra*). As *all*-receiving it becomes stamped or in-formed by all sorts of intelligible paradigms so that it serves as the receptacle for the formation of things, the *wherein* of their generation and the *whence* of their passing. But in itself, *chōra* is neither intelligible (in the order of 'being', the *ideas*) nor sensible (in order of 'becoming', the copies) (52A–C). Belonging to neither of the two genres—intelligible-formal or sensible-material—and lacking its own identity, *chōra* remains undetermined, characterless, formless, amorphous (*amorphon*) (50E). Eugene Fink thus characterized *chōra* as 'the dark nocturnal space-matter of the universe' (*die dunkle, nächtige Raum-Materie des Weltalls*). While stressing its all-embracing and nurturing nature as 'the great mother..."earth"' (*die Große Mutter, die 'Erde'*), Fink also characterizes it as 'chaos' (*das Chaos*).[29] But

---

28 Hans-Georg Gadamer, *Dialogue and Dialectic: Eight Hermeneutical Studies on Plato*, trans. P Christopher Smith (New Haven: Yale University Press, 1980), 174–75.
29 Eugene Fink, *Zur ontologischen Frühgeschichte von Raum-Zeit-Bewegung* (The Hague: Martinus Nijhoff, 1957), 187–88. Here we might mention the etymological link between the Greek terms, *chōra* and *chaos* (χάος). The latter derives from the verb *chainō* (χαίνω) for 'opening', and in Hesiod's *Theogony*, *chaos* still means 'chasm' rather than simply 'disorder'. See Max Jammer, *Concepts of Space* (Cambridge, Massachusetts: Harvard University Press, 1970), 9, and F M Cornford, *Principium Sapientiae* (New York: Harper & Row, 1965), 194 with n 1. Also see Edward Casey, *Fate of Place* (Berkeley: University of California Press, 1997), 345, n 13.

it would be good to remember that *chaos* for the most ancient of Greeks meant 'chasm', and implied an opening. Within its formlessness—the empty opening of a formless space—*chōra* makes room for things, clearing space to be occupied by whatever *becomes*. We might point out here the verb form of *chōra*, *chōreō* (χωρέω), which along with the sense of being in flux, has the sense of making room for another by giving way or withdrawing.[30] In such a way it provides an *abode* (*hedra*, ἕδρα) to all insofar as they are generated. As the *wherein* and *whence* of every *this* and *that*, *chōra* withdraws from any designation as *this* or *that*.

Nishida's dialectic of negation is predicated upon that amorphous nothingness—the *chōratic* nature—of place. The *chōratic* open in Nishida translates into the place (*basho*) delimited by nothing (*mu*). Nishida thus refers to Plato's *chōra* when first formulating his concept of place (see Z3 415). Like *chōra*, Nishida's *basho* at its most concrete level eludes positive description, and yet in its very *no-thingness*, opens a space for things determined and differentiated from one another and envelops them. It recedes into the dark to make room for the objects of our attention. Although some translators of Nishida have rendered the term *basho* into the Greek-English *topos*, and occasionally into the Latin *locus*, and while certainly Nishida himself also refers to Aristotle's conception of the soul as a '*topos* of forms' (Z3 419),[31] the sense of *basho* is truly

---

30 On this see Sallis, *Chorology*, 118.
31 See Aristotle's *On the Soul* (*De Anima*), 429A 15, in *The Basic Works of Aristotle*, ed. Richard McKeon (New York: Random House, 1941), 589. See also *Metaphysics* 1032A35–B1 (*Basic Works*, 792) where he speaks of the artist's soul as wherein the form of artificial products (the essence of each thing) lie; and see *De Anima* 406A16–20 (*Basic Works*, 543) where he speaks of the soul as itself having a place (*topos*).

closer to *chōra* than to *topos*. In general for the ancient Greeks, *topos* is the physical location that a material thing happens to occupy at the moment and that is independent of its being. *Chōra* on the other hand is the field giving room for such localities and providing the contextual significance for things. As such it is ontologically essential to *what* the thing is. Plato himself makes the distinction when he speaks of *chōra*'s thrashing motion whereby things therein are settled into their distinct *topoi* (52E–53A).[32] *Chōra* in its ontological sense as essential to the formation of beings is thus closer in significance to Nishida's notion of place than is *topos*.

---

32 To be more precise: through *chōra*'s violent thrashing motion bodies (*sōmata*) are separated out, the dense and heavy sinking down and the light and rare floating upward, each to its own place (*topos*) to settle (52E–53A). Nor should Plato's *chōra* be conflated with Aristotle's *topos* from the *Physics* as John Sallis (*Chorology*, 115) warns. There have been numerous studies on this *chōra-topos* distinctin that Nishida scholars who wish to translate *basho* as *topos* ought to be aware of: Ed Casey, *Fate of Place*; Ed Casey, 'Smooth Spaces and Rough-edged Places'; John Sallis, *Chorology*; and most notably Augustin Berque, 'Overcoming Modernity, Yesterday and Today', *Journal of East Asian Studies* 1.1 (2002): 89–102; 'Offspring of Watsuji's Theory of Milieu (*Fūdo*)', *GeoJournal* 60.4 (2004): 389–96; 'The Ontological Structure of Mediance as a Ground of Meaning in Architecture' in Tony Atkin & Joseph Rykwert, eds, *Structure and Meaning in Human Settlements* (Philadelphia: University of Pennsylvania Museum of Archaeology and Anthropology, 2005), 97–105; and *Fūdogaku josetsu—bunka o futatabi shizen ni, shizen o futatabi bunka ni*, trans. Nakayama Gen (Tokyo: Chikuma shobō, 2002) [trans. of *Écoumène: Introduction à l'étude des milieux humains* (Paris: Éditions Belin, 2000)]. Berque in turn cites Jean-François Pradeau, 'Être quelque part, occuper une place. *Topos* et *chōra* dans le *Timée*' ['Being Somewhere and Occupying a Place: *Topos* and *Chōra* in the *Timaeus*], *Les Études philosophiques*, vol. 3 (1995); Luc Brisson, *Le Même el l'autre dans la structure ontologique du Timée. Un commentaire systématique du Timée de Platon* (Sankt Augustin: Akademia Verlag, 1994); Alain Boutot, *Heidegger et Platon. Le problème du nihilisme* (Paris: Presses Universitaires de France, 1987).

Yet we also need acknowledge a difference between Plato's *chōra* and Nishida's development of it as *basho*. *Chōra* in Plato despite its status as a *triton genos* is not neutral. It is a receptacle for the *ideas*. Hence Plato likens *chōra* to the mother *vis-à-vis* the true being (*ontōs on*) of the *ideas*—or the *demiourgos* who handles them—as the father impregnating her, with *genesis* as their child (50D)—the archetypal image of Heaven the Father and Mother Earth. But this is precisely what led to the Aristotelian duality of form-matter and eventually its Kantian reformulation in epistemological terms that Nishida wants to overcome. On this account, Nishida expressed dissatisfaction with the ancient Greeks' failure to attribute any 'logical independence' to their notion of 'place' (Z7 223). For Nishida, *basho*—instead of being on the mere receiving end of formation— is *self*-forming. Its formlessness is a living creativity that forms itself. Nishida calls it a self-forming formlessness. It is in this sense that it is a nothing (*mu*) that gives rise to being (*yū*). *Basho forms itself via* the inter-determinations of things for which it makes room. In distinction from Plato's place as receptacle, Nishida's version of *chōra* is *self*-formative but *via* its individual elements, whereby the transcendent, the universal, is in fact immanent as their very *place*, a self-negating nothing that allows, by making-room, for their self- and co-determinations. In contrast to Plato's hierarchical dualism that subordinates *chōra* as receptacle, *chōra*'s status as a *triton genos* is amplified in Nishida as truly neutral and indefinable. In its nature of giving-place to the various inter-relations between opposites—such as form/idea and matter—without itself being subject to the laws it situates,³³ Nishida's *basho*, as an *empty* or *formless place*, is *chōratic* in precisely that sense.

If we are to look back at that *chōra* in light of Nishida's dialectic of contradictory self-identity, Jacques Derrida who most certainly was unaware of Nishida's appropriation, nevertheless comes close to Nishida's conception when he remarks that Plato's *chōra* seems to defy that either-or 'logic of non-contradiction', 'the logic of binarity'.³⁴ For as a *triton genos* (52A), the essential space standing *behind* and *enveloping* both being (*ideas*) and becoming (*images*, things), *chōra* is *neither* of the immutable intelligibles *nor* of the becoming and corruptible sensibles; *neither* being *qua* universal transcendent paradigm *nor* becoming-and-unbecoming beings *qua* particulars in-formed by or copying the universal paradigm; *neither* intelligible being *nor* sensible being. As a dark 'beyond' that gives place to their oppositions, it is in *excess*, irreducible, to either opposites.³⁵ As neither sensible nor intelligible, it then is *beyond* sense and meaning. Only from and within it, can their cleavage, including also that between body and mind, '*have and take* place'.³⁶

---

33 And that is how Jacques Derrida characterizes *chōra*. See his 'Khōra' in *On the Name* (Stanford: Stanford University Press, 1995), 90.
34 Ibid., 89.
35 The expression *epekeina tēs ousias* (επεκεινα της ουσιας), 'beyond being', was used by Socrates in the Republic to refer to to *agathon* (το αγαωον), 'the good'. Derrida however points out the possibility of extending the expression to *chōra*. He bases this on a passage where Socrates speaks of how the liberated prisoner, having exited the cave, could turn his gaze upward and 'be able to look upon the sun—not in its appearances [...] or in some other base [*hedra*], but the sun itself by itself in its own *chōra* [...] and behold how it is' (Republic 516B). On this see Sallis, 113-14, n. 23; and Derrida, 'Tense' in *The Path of Archaic Thinking: Unfolding the Work of John Sallis*, ed. Kenneth Maly (Albany: SUNY, 1995), 73-74.
36 Derrida, *On the Name*, 103; see also 92–93.

In its withdrawing that makes room, it perpetually slips *beyond* any reduction to the presence of an *eidos*. As an *excess* it is ontologically 'nothing', preceding all beings and allowing for all such binary or dialectical determinations. Nishida's *basho*, as itself absolutely nothing (*zettai mu*) that enfolds every opposition is *chōratic* in exactly that way, slipping away from any law of contradiction that would reduce it to exclusively being or non-being.

In its movement of clearing space for the happening thing-events, *chōra* is dynamic, not static. Everything happens in relation to everything else, near and far, in its contextual implacement. Things are predicated upon the space wherein they belong, their concrete place. But those environing or contextualizing conditions continually recede the further we inquire after them, without ever revealing any absolute answer or final principle that explains the *reason* for the way things ultimately *are*. The clearing continually recedes into the darkness of in-definition. And hence the 'absolute' for Nishida is ultimately nothing or a place delimited by absolutely nothing. This idea echoes *chōra*'s rejection of either-or logic, concurring with its ambiguity as the *wherein* of all beings and their opposites. For as the place wherein everything is marked but which itself remains unmarked, *chōra* is a place without a place, an un-implaced—even if irreplaceable—place.[37] Within that *chōra* as its place the medial body extends our limits through our *chiasmatic* interactions with environing nature. The human body is itself implaced, contextualized, horizoned, within, to mirror, the world of meanings and its further implacement within an ever-receding and

---

37 Derrida speaks of *chōra* as an 'irreplaceable and unplaceable place'. See Derrida, *On the Name*, 111.

endless amorphous *chōra* sinking into the earth. Instead of simply being projectors of meaning upon the world, we are born into that world of pre-given meanings receding into non-meaning. Meanings are contextualized and these contexts are themselves contextualized by the succession of further hidden contexts withdrawing from our grasp. As meaning-giving and -receiving subjects, we are thrown into or find ourselves already implaced within that pre-contextualizing environment, enveloping the flux of contextualized realities. But eventually the contexts and meanings sink into the a-meaning of nature, earth, contingency, finitude with which we must come to terms. Within that *chiasmatic chōra*, what is immediately present to our embodied being is but a drop in the ocean, and yet it mirrors and expresses the ocean, itself uncontextualizable, beyond meaning or purpose, with neither *archē* nor *telos*, neither beginning nor end.

If *chiasma* expresses the over-determinate aspect of Nishida's matter of thinking, *chōra* expresses its under-determinate aspect. Its indetermination is what refuses reduction to *archai* and *teloi*, principles and ends, or to any terms of opposition. Rather in its self-withdrawal, self-negation, it provides a clearing, a space for the *chiasmatic* unraveling of the many. The unfolding it enfolds is, as Nishida states, 'a determination without determiner' (*genteisurumono naki gentei* 限定するものなき限定) (Z6 15, 20–21, 116, 149, 162; Z7 12, 205). Even while nurturing the generation of things, *chōra* undermines any claim to a first substance or the hegemony of a universal First. Only when we understand the universal precisely *in light of* that an-ontological *chōratic* opening or self negation *qua place*, in its formless nothingness, can the idea of a universality—as in Nishida's dialectical universal—permit the irreducible singularity of individuals. Hegel had inherited the primacy of the *idea* from Plato as what in-forms, orders, the material of world history. Nishida, by taking-off from—and developing—*chōra* rather than the *ideas* in Plato, hoped to overcome that dichotomy between form and matter and the ensuing hierarchy with his notion of a self-forming formlessness, a place enfolding its own forms. In opposition to the *idealism* of Plato and Hegel, or more precisely, their *idea-logy* (*logos* of the *idea*/s), Nishida thus puts forth what we might call a *chorology*.[38] It serves as a dark undertow that pulls apart and tears asunder metaphysical tendencies. John Sallis has remarked that *chōra* both originates metaphysics and exposes it to its abyss; it engulfs metaphysics as its beginning and end.[39] Within the space it clears, metaphysical 'firsts'—substances, principles, absolutes—are erected but also toppled. Hence we question the adequacy of a language of dialectical logic that borrows Hegelian terminology to express Nishida's matter of thought, the *chiasmatic chōra*. In concrete terms, however, I think we might develop Nishida's idea further by underscoring the original pre-Platonic Greek meaning of *chōra* in the sense of 'region' or 'country', our natural environment that sinks its roots into the very earth that provides a space for our dwelling. In that respect *chōra* is abysmal yet truly concrete, ground and unground.

---

38 I am borrowing this term from John Sallis' discussion of the *chōra* in his *Chorology*.
39 See Sallis, *Chorology*, 123.

CONCLUSION: CHIASMATIC CHŌRA

Chōra both supports, or rather engulfs in its gaping abyss, *and* is constituted by its *chiasma*. Nishida's mature thought—'the dialectic of place' (*basho no benshōhō* 場所の弁証法)—entails both together as a *chiasmatic chōra*. *Chōra* engulfs and supports in its abyss an economy of generation-and-dissolution whereupon quasi-substances and apparent principles are generated and cease as singular constellations in *chiasmatic* concurrences of manifold forces and dimensions. This concrete *chiasma* of what Nishida calls 'absolute dialectic' cannot be expressed adequately in terms of Hegelian dialectics. And *place* in its nature as a self-withdrawing *chōra* that founds this dialectic—enfolding and unfolding its *chiasma* that in turn determines its shape—also escapes the grasp of a conceptual systematic such as that of Hegel's self-conceiving concept or self-knowing spirit. The self-determination of the (under)determined *chōra* is a *chiasma* of (over)inter-determinations, a perpetually reconfiguring *chiasmatic chōra*, the sheer complexity of which undermines any final *Aufhebung*. What we have here then is a *chiasmology* in opposition to Aristotelian *ousiology* and a *chorology* in distinction from Platonist and Hegelian *idea-logy* (i.e., their idealism). And if it is the principles—rules for thought—that decide what *is* and *is-not*, *chiasmatic chōra* irreducible—in its over- and under-determinations—to being or non-being, proves to be the *an*-ontological origin of both *on* and *mēon* (being and non-being). Both *chōra* and *chiasma* here work together to undermine, in Nishida's system of in-completion, any semblance to a metaphysical self-closure under the postulation of an absolute—whether as *idea* or concept or *Geist* or substance. It is the very matter of Nishida's own thinking that has undermined his own repeated attempts to grasp it under the structure of a completed system once-and-for-all. Never reaching its end, his philosophy is thus parabolical. To read Nishida in such terms allows us to bring him into a more intimate dialogue with the more recent post-Hegelian thinkers of the West in the twentieth and twenty first centuries, who in countering the *ousiology* of traditional western metaphysics have also been attending to place, *chōra*, *chiasma*, and related or similar issues.

What are the more practical implications and relevance of *chiasmatic chōra* for us today as the human world becomes globalized—a situation where its apparent universality upon the global surface is countered by an encounter with its ever-more explicit *other/s*? The world today in its globalization is unfolding its *chiasmatic* nature as a place of manifold contradictions and oppositions. *Chōratic* indetermination manifests itself in its expanse permitting the multiple ways of being, dwelling, living, speaking, thinking, doing—the 'American way', the Christian way, Eastern Orthodoxy, the Eastern traditions, Confucian propriety, punk rock subculture, the *sangha*, communism, the *ummah*, online shopping, etc. These multiple ways encounter one another and contend, inter-determine, and intertwine in a *chiasma* over the globe but also within a continent, a civilization, a nation, a city, a webpage, even within a single human individual, to in turn open new configurations and possibilities. The experience is destabilizing and yet can also be exhilarating, enlightening, freeing. It can also be violent and destructive. Amidst alterations, mutations, and conflicts of traditions and horizons, it may do us well to bear in mind the indefinite and irreducible expanse *wherein* we *all are* in *co-implacement* amidst differences. The *chiasma* is the unfolding of that *chōratic* expanse.

We recall that for Nishida it is the world's non-substantiality as the self-formation of formlessness that permits individuals' self-determinations. The nothing clears space for our positive self-determination. The individual is simultaneously grounded and ungrounded upon the world of implacement in its place of nothing, giving us leeway to act freely upon the world. The world's dialectic of manifold inter-determination is such that the vertical determination moves not only top down but in reverse to move bottom up. What on the vertical level is the world's self-determination, on the horizontal level means the interdetermination among individuals, an interdetermination that in the reverse vertical direction determines the worlds as a whole. Mutually independent as individuals, yet at the same time we are interdependent. This *chiasma* of interdetermination is predicated upon the indetermination of the cleared expanse, *chōra*, wherein the world is built. This *nothing* of the world's un/ground, sinking into the earth and beyond, clears room for our autonomy, coexistence, and plurality—something, however, that we would have to work to realize, especially in the face of a domineering capitalist imaginary claiming global legitimacy for its consumer (pseudo-)culture.

Neither can we deny here that tension involved in the interaction between humanity and nature—a certain resistance that can turn violent, whether in man's violation of nature or in nature's obstruction of human constructions, perhaps even escalating to a circle of mutual destruction, e.g., the H-bomb, massive hurricanes and tsunamis. But the notion of our place of dwelling as *chiasma* and *chōra*, by rejecting the culture-nature dichotomy, underscores our holistic symbiosis with the earth as the anontological (un)ground and opening for our co-existence in a concrete milieu with one another and with nature. It is this earth, the un/ground, as our ultimate contextual *wherein* that provides a clearing for co-dwelling and mutual encounter with one's *other*—other human beings, other species, nature itself untrammeled by humanity, the *other* as *also* our *co*-being—that we must acknowledge today if we are to co-exist authentically, that is exist freely *with* our global neighbors and *with* the surrounding nature.

The Alchemical Chiasmus

*Creativity, Counter-Stretched Harmony,
& Divine Self-Perception*

AARON CHEAK & SABRINA DALLA VALLE[1]

*Tu ne me chercherais pas,
si tu ne m'avais trouvé.*
'You would not have sought me,
if you had not found me'.[2]
—PASCAL

¶ THE WORD CHIASMUS comes from the Greek word *chiazō*, 'to shape like the letter x'.[3] A chiasmus usually describes rhetorical forms involving inversion and reciprocity, and perhaps the oldest and most immediate chiasmic structures are those found in the fragments of Heraclitus:

---

[1] The key concepts and substantial content of the present essay were fleshed out by Sabrina Dalla Valle and myself in August 2011 and were consolidated over the following year. Thanks are due to Rod Blackhirst, Dan Mellamphy, and Patrick Lee Miller, whose ideas and works proved particularly influential at the time. —AC.
[2] Blaise Pascal, *Pensées*, ed. Léon Brunschvicg (Paris: Hachette, 1897), 553.
[3] In Greek, the 'x' is represented by the letter *chi* (χ or X), which can be transliterated as *kh-* or *ch-* and has the phonetic value of an uvular fricative (as in German *Bach*, Scottish *loch*, etc.) The character gives rise to the Roman and thus English letter 'x', which, while using the same character, has a different phonetic value (*-ks*, in Greek, ξ).

ἀθάνατοι θνητοί,
θνητοὶ ἀθάντατοι,
ζῶντες τὸν ἐκείνων θάνατον,
τὸν δὲ ἐκείνων βίον τεθνεῶτες

Mortals are immortals,
and immortals are mortals,
living the others' death,
and dying the others' life.[4]

At the heart of the chiasmus is thus a paradox—two opposite conditions are placed in seeming contradiction—yet both are integral to each other's truth.

Mortals are immortals. A.	Immortals are mortals. B.
B. Living the mortal's death.	A. Dying the immortal's life.

The x, of course, is but a symbol. In reality, the chiasmus must be perceived as a *continuous* process, much like the mathematical symbol for infinity or endlessness embodied in the figure eight—∞—or the simple but deceptive 'twist in reality' that gives rise to the Möbius strip. The circulation of inversion and reciproc-

---

4 Heraclitus, fragment 62 (Hippolytus, *Refutation of all Heresies*, IX, 10, 6).

ity thus describes a perfect dialectic of opposites.[5]

According to Miller, the chiasmus 'threatens to violate the principle of non-contradiction whenever its components are conjoined and opposed, whether as contraries or contradictories':

> This happens often in the Heraclitean aphorisms, but nowhere more flagrantly than in the following, which we shall eventually call the principle of the chiasmus: 'wholes and not-wholes, convergent divergent, consonant dissonant, from all things one and from one all things'.[6]

What is more, every living thing, in its comportment to all other things, naturally embodies such a relationship. Every living presence implies a counter-presence, a counter-*weaving*, of affinities and aversions, a simultaneous attraction and repulsion that, like the string of a lyre stretched between two poles, creates an inherent, yet vital, *tonos* (tone, tension). This tonification, harnessed and focused like a bow and arrow, stimulates attention and intention; awareness and will. It is both the seed and fruit of creative expression, evoking a vivifying harmony that engenders a corresponding mode of perception and consciousness.

For Heraclitus, this *tonos* or tension is inherent to the constitution of reality. To illustrate the unity of harmony and death generated by this tension, he used the twin instruments of Apollo and Artemis—the bow and lyre:

---

[5] Here we see immediately that the chiasmic structure indicates a reciprocal relationship, following the form A:B:B:A, as in Plato's *Timaeus*. See also Patrick Lee Miller, *Becoming God: Pure Reason in Early Greek Philosophy* (New York: Continuum, 2011), 7 ff.

[6] Miller, *Becoming God*, 8.

οὐ ξυνιασιν ὅκως διαφερόμενον ἑωυτῷ ξυμφέρεται·
παλίντονος ἁρμονίη ὅκωσπερ τόξου καὶ λύρης.

They do not apprehend how being brought apart it is brought together with itself: there is a counterstretched harmony, like the bow and the lyre.[7]

For here reality is a process rather than a fixed form, and inherent to this process is the principle of 'return by departure' (being brought together by being brought apart). What seems, paradoxically, to be a process of becoming distant from the 'centre' or 'principle' (origin, divinity, ground of being) is in fact an activity of this centre that fulfils its potential, and by doing so, ultimately leads back to itself. Like the bow, it has to be stretched away from itself in order to fulfil itself; that is to say, in order to harness the higher state of tensility that lies latent in the wood, the wood must be bent back against itself. Like the lyre, the potential harmony cannot exist without the tensility of string and wood creating tone (*tonos*), for there is no tone without stretching or tension (*tonos* comes from *tenein*, 'to stretch'). A true chiasmus, therefore, is always a vital, tensile interweaving. It is both the warp and weft of reality, as well as its animating *puissance*.

THE ANIMA MUNDI

Content mirrors form. The chiasmic connection between immortality and mortality that we meet in Heraclitus is not merely coin-

---

[7] Heraclitus, fragment 51 (Hyppolytus, *Ref.* IX, 9, 1). Cf. fragment 65: Τὸ ὄνομα του τόξου εἶναι η ζωή, αλλά το έργο του είναι ο θάνατος (The name of the bow is life, but its work is death).

cidental. What we find here is more explicitly mirrored in perhaps the most difficult passage in Plato—*Timaeus* 35A–37B—in which the formation of the World Soul (*psychē kosmou, anima mundi*) is described as the very *link* between the eternal and the transient.[8] In this most alchemical of Plato's dialogues, the indivisible (the 'circle of the same') is linked to the divisible ('the circle of difference') via what he calls 'the best of possible bonds' (*desmōn de kallistos*).[9] When the two circles, which do not want to join, are united, their point of union forms an x or cross (*chi*). This chiasmus defines the paradoxical juncture of spirit and matter, fire and earth. It is the spiritual point in the material world and the material point in the spiritual world.

In Platonic cosmology, the demiurge or divine artisan brings the infinite and the finite together to form a single point, and the result is the World Soul. In other words, this absolute chiasmic juncture is the very thing that animates the world (*anima mundi*). The world soul, moreover, is mirrored in the Platonic conception of the embodied soul, which is precisely conceived as a *mean term*

---

8 For a history of the idea of the World Soul and its continued significance, see David Fideler's contribution to the present volume, and his recent book, *Restoring the Soul of the World: Our Living Bond with Nature's Intelligence* (Rochester, Vermont: Inner Traditions, 2015).

9 Plato, *Timaeus*, 31B–C: 'Now that which comes to be must have bodily form, and be both visible and tangible, but nothing could ever become visible apart from fire, nor tangible without something solid, nor solid without earth. That is why, as he came to put the body of the universe together, the Demiurge came to make it out of fire and earth. But it isn't possible to combine two things well all by themselves, without a third; there has to be some bond between the two that unites them. Now the best bond is the one that really and truly makes a unity of itself together with the things bonded by it, and this in the nature of things is best accomplished by proportion' (trans. modified after Zeyl).

between the divine and the human. It puts human perception in a privileged but also *torn* condition, enabling perspective on both the metaphysical and the physical worlds.

Through its 'counter-stretched harmony', the taut and tensile human *psychē* mirrors the macrocosmic chiasmus. Herein, the tension that mitigates against unity is secretly vital to its greater integrity. Like the dissonant seventh in musical harmony, tension anticipates the resolution of the fundamental *tonos* in the octave, while simultaneously maintaining perfect distance and equilibrium. Like the divine artisan, the human soul must not only wed the eternal to the transient, it must comprehend life's grandest structures through its most contradictory details. Like the artisan, the artist embraces contradiction to encompass the feeling of infinity.

The counter-stretched nature of creation was sensed very keenly in modern times by Andrei Tarkovsky, the great Russian filmmaker who likened film to 'sculpting in time', and directing to literally being able to 'separate light from darkness' and 'dry land from the waters' (Genesis 1: 9–18).[10] 'The work of art', remarks Tarkovsky, 'lives and develops, like any other natural organism, through the conflict of opposing principles'.[11]

> Hideousness and beauty are contained within each other. This prodigious paradox, in all its absurdity, leavens life itself, and in art makes that wholeness in which harmony

---

10 Andrei Tarkovsky, *Sculpting in Time: Reflections on the Cinema*, trans. Kitty Hunter-Blair (New York: Alfred A Knopf, 1987), 47, 177: 'The director's power is such that it can create the illusion of him being a kind of demiurge; hence the grave temptations of his profession, which can lead him very far in the wrong direction'.
11 Ibid., 39.

and tension are unified. The image makes palpable a unity in which manifold different elements are contiguous and reach over into each other. [...] The idea of infinity cannot be expressed in words or even described, but it can be apprehended through art, which makes infinity tangible. The absolute is only attainable through faith and in the creative act.[12]

Proceeding through opposition, art *makes infinity tangible*. All authentic *ars*, all traditional *technē*, seek to render the universal creative act present through finite creation. Here, we take *ars* and *technē* in their archaic senses, in which both 'art' and 'craft/technology' were not dualised, but were each seen to participate in the divine intelligence (*nous, epistemē, scientia*), and by virtue of this were distinguished from artless labour (*atechnos tribē*).[13] According to the medieval dictum *ars sine scientia nihil* (art is nothing without knowledge), no separation was made between a work of art *per se* and ordinary, 'utilitarian' objects, as is the case in the modern world; rather, handcrafted objects were not soullessly manufactured, but *transformed* into works of art through the very act of *poēsis* (creation). They were vivified, hence life-giving. The false dichotomy between high art and low technology has come about precisely because manufactured objects (*cheirotechnē*) are no longer made by hand: they have lost their soul, their animating connection to the human and transcendent. As the Alsatian Hermetic philosopher, René Schwaller de Lubicz, once remarked:

---

12 Tarkovsky, *Sculpting in Time*, 38–39.
13 Ananda Coomaraswamy, 'Athena and Hephaistos', in *What is Civilisation? And Other Essays* (Great Barrington: Lindisfarne Press, 1989), 184.

If someone were to tell you that mechanised civilisation clouds the soul, this would be an affirmation without practical impact. On the other hand, if I say to you that mechanised civilisation clouds and even kills consciousness, you will comprehend this warning: if between yourself and the object of your labour you interpose an automatic tool which eliminates your will and above all your sensibility, all living contact between you and the fashioned material is cut off. The artisan no longer 'feels' (*sent*) and no longer comprehends the wood, the leather, the metal, his work is inanimate; it cannot emanate nor radiate any life for it has not received any. You must then resort to analyses, to statistical studies of the qualities of the material relinquished to the automatism of the machine, for you have stretched a veil between yourself and the thing; and although the thing subsists, you—the conscious living being—lose your life by suffocating your consciousness. It is the same with the doctor, who must sympathetically feel (*éprouver*) his patient's illness, or otherwise become a mechanic. Observe the phases of history: the most fruitful, the most genial and the most 'living' epochs have always had a flourishing community of artisans. The Consciousness of a people can only be renewed through the crafts and not through doctrines. Mechanised civilisation is the agony of the world.[14]

Plato, as Coomaraswamy reminds us, 'knows nothing of our distinction of fine from applied arts. For him painting and agricul-

---

14 René Schwaller de Lubicz, *Verbe Nature*, §38 (trans. modified after Lawlor).

ture, music and carpentry and pottery are all equally kinds of poetry or making' (*poēsis*).[15]

Ars and *technē* thus conceived are not merely mirrors or simulacra, but *instruments* and *instances* of creation, of making infinity tangible. Creation, in this sense, is regarded as continuous and ever-present, and all true creativity is thus *participation* in the ever-presence of origin. The artist creates an image of the absolute, according to Tarkovsky, and 'through the image is sustained an awareness of the infinite: the eternal within the finite, the spiritual within matter, the limitless given form'.[16] The animating paradox at the heart of life is thus the hidden ferment through which harmony and tension are unified.

THE RECIPROCAL PERCEPTION OF REALITY

At the heart of the chiasmic idea is a 'metaphysics of perception' in which human perception becomes an instrument of divine self-perception. 'The eye with which I see God is the same eye with which God sees me', Eckhart famously remarked.[17] 'I was a hidden treasure, and I desired to be known, so I created creatures, in order to become in them the object of my knowledge', runs an Islamic hadith central to the cosmogony of Ibn al-Arabī.[18] What we have here is not a matter of turning away from the senses in order

15 Ananda Coomaraswamy, 'Why Exhibit Works of Art?', in *Christian and Oriental Philosophy of Art* (New York: Dover, 1990), 9.
16 Tarkovsky, *Sculpting in Time*, 37.
17 Meister Eckhart, *Deutsche Predigten und Traktate*, ed., trans., Josef Quint, (München: Hanser, 1995), 216 (Predigt 13, Qui audit me): 'Das Auge, in dem ich Gott sehe, das ist dasselbe Auge, darin mich Gott sieht'.
18 Henry Corbin, *Alone with the Alone: Creative Imagination in the Sūfism of Ibn 'Arabī* (Princeton, New Jersey: Princeton University Press, 1969), 114 ff.

to attain transcendence, but of *engaging* and using the senses properly in order to attain a perceptually 'grounded' transcendence; an *embodied* liberation (*jivanmukti*) in which we both embrace and supersede our finite individuality.[19] Here, reality *perceives itself* through the vehicle of human consciousness, and reciprocally, human consciousness *participates* in the self-perception of unrestricted reality.

Both 'poles' give something to the greater integrity of the whole. As Rudolf Steiner points out in two remarkably chiasmic poems, the earthly or material pole of reality provides the seed of the spiritual pole, while the spiritual pole provides the seed of the earthly. The first line of each poem begins:

Im Geiste lag der Keim meines Leibes [...]
In meinem Leibe liegt des Geistes Keim.
In the spirit lay the germ of my body [...]
In my body lies the germ of the spirit.[20]

For Steiner, a deeper world existed behind both the world of the senses and the realm of the soul. Both the life of the soul—the intensity of our emotions, impulses, and desires—and the boundaries of the senses proper, confine us. 'One must give up one's [ordinary] existence in order to [truly] exist',[21] remarks Steiner. Following Goethe, he advocated the refinement, indeed *distillation*, of emotion and sense, dream and waking, in order to free one's being

---

19 See especially Christopher Bamford, 'Common Sense: An Interview with Peter Kingsley', in *Parabola* 31.1 (Spring, 2006): 24-30.
20 Rudolf Steiner, *Guidance in Esoteric Training* (London: Rudolf Steiner Press, 1998), 70.
21 Ibid., 62.

from its internal and external boundaries, thus liberating it into a deeper, more authentic experience of reality.[22]

In Heideggerian terms, one must allow pure authenticity (*Eigentlichkeit*) to arise between the godly and the counter-godly. Authenticity, for Heidegger, unconceals the concealed, rendering the eternal godhead in us diaphanous. This diaphanous juncture of the godly and the counter-godly, the eternal and the transient, is described by Heidegger as a 'ripped open cleft', which is bound together by the intimacy of their difference.[23] Rather than seeking a middle ground, each opposite evokes its counterpole: a feeling for contiguity formed from their reciprocal appropriations from one another. And it is precisely through this contiguity and counterpolarity that they find their completion. Paradoxically, each finds their individual freedom only when they let go of themselves and abandon their particularity.

To become an instrument of the chiasmic demiurge, the artisan must have the courage to open themselves up to the unknown, to become a servant to a process that is beyond them, and to embody thereby the method of nondual conjunction through a deep sense of primordial trust. Germane to this process is a mysterious element that one can never quite grasp: a *quidam*, as Samuel Beckett called it (a certain 'someone' or 'something', a *je ne sais quoi*).[24] This

---

22 Rudolf Steiner, *The Science of Knowing: Outline of the Epistemology Implicit in the Goethean World View* (Spring Valley, New York: Mercury Press, 1988), 53.
23 Martin Heidegger, 'The Origin of the Work of Art', in *Poetry, Language, Thought*, trans. Albert Hofstadter (New York: Harper & Row, 1971), 63.
24 On Samuel Beckett and the chiasmus, see Dan Mellamphy's magisterial 'Alchemical Endgame: "Checkmate" in Beckett and Eliot', in Cheak, ed., *Alchemical Traditions: From Antiquity to the Avant-Garde* (Melbourne: Numen, 2013), 548–638.

mysterious *quidam* lives not in ordinary feeling, but in a sensitivity for what is simultaneously present but *missing*: what is both ever-present yet ever-absent to the deeper constitution of reality. To sense this ever-presence and ever-absence requires a certain temperament, or conjunction of temperaments—what Ezra Pound referred to as an 'aristocracy of emotion'. It is precisely through this aristocracy of emotion, this refined sensitivity, that one intuits the shifting mystery *behind* the chiasmus: the *quidam* that *conceals through revelation* and *reveals through concealment*.

For ultimately, this dialectic of revelation and concealment is precisely a crossing, a concretisation of the spirit, a *salt* in the alchemical sense (a neutralisation reaction between sulphur and mercury, 'acid' and a 'base'). It locks and unlocks, binds and unbinds, dissolves and coagulates. The cross of human incarnation both 'crucifies' us to earth and provides a vehicle of transcendence. This leads to the realisation that liberation is achieved *in* life (rather than beyond life). And yet, what is being distilled in the crucible of existence has already been achieved *beyond* life. It is already eternal. As such, we are fertile earth for living impulses that are at once our own unique creations as they are *conduits* for something that precedes, animates, and transcends us. As the Prussian poet and phenomenologist, Jean Gebser, points out, this conduit is no less than integral consciousness itself: the crystalline *Diaphainon* (transparency, *Durchsichtigkeit*) through which both darkness and light, origin and *telos*, are rendered 'ever-present'.[25] By

---

25 Origin, synonymous for Gebser with the wellsprings of all consciousness (*Ur-sprung*, the 'primordial leap'), is not an event fixed in the past, but an ever-present spiritual process continually available to an intensified (tonified) awareness.

rendering origin present through the mirror of the *anima mundi*, human consciousness itself becomes an active chiasmus and thus participates in the *empsychosis*—the ensouling—of the world. All embodiment, all creation, thus becomes a vehicle for the catalytic vivification of the cosmos.

In contrast to positivist epistemology, which focuses only on the one-sided, empirical particulars (asserting an epistemology in which only what is measurable is real), the chiasmic apperception is holarchical, originating from and culminating in an immediate gnosis of the whole: 'It appears as a revelation, as a momentary, passionate wish to grasp intuitively and at a stroke all the laws of this world—its beauty and ugliness, its compassion and cruelty, its infinity and limitations', remarks Tarkovsky.[26] There is still an empiricism at play here, but it is a 'delicate empiricism'—a *zarte Empirie*, as Goethe called it—which is too rigorous for poets and artists, but too subtle for physicists and scientists, and thus liable to be overlooked by both. But it is precisely this subtle yet tensile chiasmus of the two temperaments that is required. And here we must remember that the original idea behind an 'experiment' was precisely this: a juncture of both subjectivity and objectivity—the desire to *experience* the reality for oneself—and this juncture of the objective and subjective poles of experience is germane to the Latin word *experimentum* itself, which means both 'experiment' and 'experience'. It is for this reason that Goethe described the experiment as a mediator (*Vermittlung*) between subject and object.

---

26 Tarkovsky, *Sculpting in Time*, 37.

Here we are in the presence of what German Romantics such as Franz von Baader called a 'reciprocal engendering' of reality.[27] When the counterstretched chiasmus is struck between human perception and divine perception, a synergistic rapport is achieved. In such moments of exchange—when perception and presence permeate each other—the harmonies of the world soul and the human soul are awakened, both despite *and* because of their inherent tensilities. 'The principle of the chiasmus', remarks Miller, 'thus reveals itself as the logos not only of understanding, but ultimately of divine self-knowledge'.[28] Consciousness is intensified into a diaphanous integrum, and the body that bears this awareness is fundamentally transfigured.

---

27 See Antoine Faivre, *Theosophy, Imagination, Tradition: Studies in Western Esotericism*, trans. Christine Rhone (Albany: SUNY, 2000), 143 ff., 158 ff.
28 Miller, *Becoming God*, 38.

CONTRIBUTORS

AARON CHEAK, PHD, is a scholar of comparative religion, philosophy, and esotericism. He received his doctorate in Religious Studies from the University of Queensland in 2011 for his work on French Hermetic philosopher, René Schwaller de Lubicz, and is the current president of the International Jean Gebser Society. Cheak is the author and editor of *Alchemical Traditions: From Antiquity to the Avant-Garde* (2013), and has appeared in *The Journal for the Academic Study of Magic* (2004), *Occult Traditions* (2012), and *Clavis: Cipher and Stone* (2014). In 2014 he founded Rubedo Press with Dr Jennifer Zahrt, where in addition to *Diaphany* he oversees the Panopolis Project (Critical Forays into the Hellenistic-Egyptian Alchemical World). Outside the academy, Aaron has been trained in the preparation of spagyric elixirs in the Albertus tradition (Paracelsus College; Spagyricus Institute), and is a practitioner within the Nyingma and Kagyu lineages of Vajrayana Buddhism. Antipodean and hyperborean, he maintains an active interest in tea, wine, poetry, typography, and alchemy.

SABRINA DALLA VALLE, MFA received her undergraduate degree from Reed College and her MFA in Writing and Consciousness from New College of California in San Francisco. Her greatest interest is in the poetic imagination as an aspect of both phenomenological perception and authentic integral expression. Her work aims to explore the 'arational', what is understood as living thinking free from both irrational faith and rational certitude. She is the author of *7 Days and Night in the Desert (Tracing the Origin)* (Kelsey Street Press, 2013, winner of best first book); 'Resignify' in *Best Poems of 2012* (Kore Press, 2013); and 'Alchemical Khiasmos' co-authored with Aaron Cheak in *Alchemical Traditions* (Numen, 2013). Her poetry and essays have been published and archived in numerous journals and venues—notably UC Berkeley Art Museum and Pacific Film Archive; University of Pennsylvania's Center for Programs in Contemporary Writing (PennSound); San Francisco State University's The Poetry Center; *New York Quarterly*; and many other small journals.

TIMOTHY ELY became a voracious reader at a young age. Painting became his primary interest just after the summer of love (1967), a time of extraordinary fertility in visual art. With an awareness that design was the grounding language, Ely pursued a degree in Fine Art. Following graduate school (MFA, Design, 1975), Ely undertook a self-motivated study of bookbinding and began to fabricate the work he is known for today: a fusion of largely English-style binding techniques with visionary drawings of an unknowable future. A reciepient of numerous awards, he travelled to Japan, Italy, and England with an NEA grant (1982), studying bookbinding and paper-making. Following this he moved to New York where he established a studio and taught at the Center for Book Arts. During this period he lectured, exhibited, and taught in Europe, Central America, and Scandinavia. He has held numerous solo exhibitions and has participated in many group exhibitions. His two most recent were at the Jundt Museum of Art and The Northwest Museum of Art and Culture. His work is collected globally and is held in public, private, and secret collections. He currently lives in Eastern Washington near the Colfax river. He is represented by Ursus Books in New York.

DAVID FIDELER has worked as an editor, college professor, educational consultant, and the director of a humanities center. He studied ancient Greek philosophy and Mediterranean religions at the University of Pennsylvania and holds a PHD in philosophy and the history of science and cosmology. David is the author of *Restoring the Soul of the World: Our Living Bond With Nature's Intelligence* (2014) (www.thesouloftheworld.com), editor of the Cosmopolis Project website (www.cosmopolisproject.org), and editor of the humanities journal *Alexandria: Cosmology, Philosophy, Myth, and Culture*. A recognized authority on the Pythagorean school, Fideler contributed encyclopedia articles on Pythagoras and Pythagoreanism to *Classical and Medieval Literature Criticism* (1997) and *The New Dictionary of the History of Ideas* (2004).

JOHN W M KRUMMEL is Associate Professor in the Department of Religious Studies at Hobart and William Smith Colleges in Geneva, New York; Assistant Editor of *The Journal of Japanese Philosophy* published by SUNY Press; and Co-Editor of *Social Imaginaries* published by Zeta Books. He has a PHD in Philosophy from the New School for Social Research and a PHD in Religion from Temple University. His dissertation at the New School was on Heidegger and Kant, while his dissertation at Temple University was on the dialectic of Nishida. He is the author of *Nishida Kitarō's Chiasmatic Chorology: Place of Dialectice, Dialectic of Place* (Bloomingotn: Indiana University Press, 2015). His writings on Heidegger, Nishida, Schürmann, and Buddhist philosophy, but also on other topics, have appeared in a variety of journals, including *Auslegung, PoMo Magazine, Dao, International Philosophical Quarterly, Existentia, Philosophy Today, Vera Lex, Journal of Chinese Philosophy, Research in Phenomenology, Philosophy East and West, Anarchist Developments in Cultural Studies*, and *Social Imaginaries*, as well as in several books as chapters. He is the co-translator of, and author of the introduction for, *Place and Dialectic: Two Essays by Nishida Kitarō* (New York: Oxford University Press, 2011). He was born and raised in Tokyo in a bilingual family.

NICOLA MASCIANDARO is Professor of English at Brooklyn College (CUNY) and a specialist in medieval literature. He is the author of *The Voice of the Hammer: The Meaning of Work in Middle English Literature* (Notre Dame, 2007) and is the founding editor of the journal *Glossator: Practice and Theory of the Commentary*. Recent works include *Dark Nights of the Universe*, co-authored with Daniel C Barber, Alexander Galloway, and Eugene Thacker (NAME, 2013), *Sufficient Unto the Day: Sermones Contra Solicitudinem* (Schism, 2014), and *Black Metal Theory: Floating Tomb*, co-authored with Edia Connole (Mimesis, 2015).

MOSELLE NITA SINGH was raised in LeClaire, Iowa, where she grew up alongside the native oak savanna and tall grass prairie her parents lovingly began regenerating when she was a child. She attributes her insight, volition, core ethics, and fundamental humanity to the experience of growing alongside the nature embedded in the land. Observing the flora and fauna were pivotal in her creative vision and her current activism in ecological regeneration. She studied anthropology at Augustana College in Rock Island, Illinois, where she wrote her contribution to *Diaphany*. She was inspired and mentored by her professor, Dr Cyrus Ali Zargar, the scholar of Sufi aesthetics. Since graduating in 2013, she has traveled to Nicaragua, India, France, and across the Midwest of the United States to work at various permaculture projects, eco-regenerative initiatives, seed banks, small-scale organic farms, and community projects, including Navdanya's Biodiversity Conservation Farm (founded by Vandana Shiva, the prominent environmental activist and physicist) and Plum Village (the meditation community of Thich Nhat Hanh, the renowned Buddhist monk and peace activist). She continues to be inspired by her travels, living simply and observing the art of the wild, never forgetting to plant seeds and trees along the way.

CONTRIBUTORS   265

DR JASON M WIRTH is professor of philosophy at Seattle University, and works and teaches in the areas of Continental Philosophy, Buddhist Philosophy, Aesthetics, and Africana Philosophy. His recent books include a monograph on Milan Kundera (*Commiserating with Devastated Things*, Fordham, 2015), *The Conspiracy of Life: Meditations on Schelling and His Time* (SUNY, 2003), a translation of the third draft of *The Ages of the World* (SUNY, 2000), the edited volume *Schelling Now* (Indiana, 2004), *Schelling's Practice of the Wild* (SUNY, 2015), the co-edited volume (with Bret Davis and Brian Schroeder), *Japanese and Continental Philosophy: Conversations with the Kyoto School* (Indiana, 2011), and *The Barbarian Principle: Merleau-Ponty, Schelling, and the Question of Nature* (SUNY, 2013). He is the associate editor and book review editor of the journal, *Comparative and Continental Philosophy* (and its attendant book series, published by Northwestern University Press). He is completing a manuscript called *Zen and Zarathustra* as well as a study of the cinema of Terrence Malick. He is a co-director of three philosophical societies: The Comparative and Continental Philosophy Circle, The Pacific Association for the Continental Tradition, and the North American Schelling Society.

ELISABET YANAGISAWA is an artist and doctoral student at the University of Gothenburg, currently completing her thesis in artistic research entitled: '*Proximus sensibilis*—The Abyss of the Surface'. Yanagisawa investigates the philosophy of matter and the principle of affect through East Asian aesthetics, focusing on the Japanese notions of *yūgen*, *wabi*, *sabi*, and *iki*. Her research deals with artistic self-cultivation and the desire of the sensible. Parallel to this, Yanagisawa explores the metaphysics of Deleuze and Spinoza for new ways of articulating the power of an animated reality through neo-materialism and ethico-aesthetics. Elisabet has a background in fashion as an independent clothing artist (1992–2000), and as lecturer in fashion and costume at Konstfack, Stockholm (2004–2009). She explores multisensibility in the aesthetics of the Way of Tea, and through the olfactory art of creating fragrances. She has held exhibitions in Japan, and has curated Japanese artists in Sweden ('Ikebana and Contemporary Plant Art', Uppsala Botanical Gardens, 2014). Elisabet has a Swedish mother and a Japanese father, and lives and works outside Stockholm, Sweden.

JENNIFER ZAHRT, PHD, writes about the history, philosophy, and epistemology of astrology, with a special focus on the German cultural sphere. Her doctoral thesis, titled *The Astrological Imaginary in Early Twentieth Century Germany* (University of California, Berkeley, 2012), concerns the ways in which astrology shaped philosophy, literature, and the arts during the Weimar Republic. Zahrt began her work as a professional editor in 2007—first, for the interdisciplinary humanities journal, *Representations* (2007–2010), then, the literary arts quarterly, *The Threepenny Review* (2011–2013), as well as the academic journal, *Culture and Cosmos* (2010–). She is the series editor for the Sophia Centre Master Monographs (Sophia Centre Press, University of Wales Trinity St David), and in 2014, Zahrt co-founded Rubedo Press with Dr Aaron Cheak. She has taught and lectured in Germany, the United Kingdom, and North America. In 2013 she translated Zoroaster's Telescope (Ouroboros Press), and her articles have appeared in *The Threepenny Review*, and *Table Talk* (Counterpoint, 2015), which she co-edited with Wendy Lesser and Mimi Chubb. Zahrt is currently working on a book titled, *Strategies of Legitimacy: Astrological Polemics in Pre-WWII Germany*. She lives in Seattle, Washington, where she serves on the Board of Trustees of Kepler College.

ILLUSTRATION CREDITS

THE FRONT AND BACK COVER IMAGES, as well as the illustrations accompanying the chapter 'Sensitive Crystalizations' are photographs of the crystallography experimentations described in that chapter, taken by Sabrina Dalla Valle; used with permission.

14, 17 SABRINA DALLA VALLE, 'Sensitive Crystallizations'.

20 PAUL KLEE (1879–1940), 'The Growth of the Night Plants', 1922; public domain.

38, 65 KANŌ SANRAKU (1559–1635), 'Set of Sliding Doors of Plum Tree', detail, early seventeenth century; public domain.

42 DONG YUAN (c. 934–c. 962), 'Dongtian Mountain Hall', National Palace Museum, Taipei; public domain.

66 'Nautilus shell', stock image purchased from graphicleftovers.com; image ID 697865, provided by David Fideler; used with permission.

74 'Pythagorean Tetractys' (diagram), provided by David Fideler; used with permission.

90 'Plato's description of the World Soul' (diagram), provided by David Fideler; used with permission.

93 'Fractal model of a maple leaf', and 'Fractal model of a coral' from Michael Barnsley, *Fractals Everywhere*, reproduced by permission of Michael Barnsley via David Fideler; 'Cross-section of a cauliflower', provided by David Fideler; used with permission.

94 TIMOTHY C ELY, *Seer*, 2014, detail; used with permission.

96 'Ely at the Drawing Board', 2011; photograph by L GERBRANDT; used with permission.

101 TIMOTHY C ELY, *Seer*, 2014, detail; used with permission.

106 TIMOTHY C ELY, *Connect the Outer Ring*, 2009, detail; used with permission.

109 TIMOTHY C ELY, *Measure of the Hypercube*, 2004, collection of Lilly Library; *Redshift*, 2007, collection of Wesleyan University; used with permission;

114 'Saint Petersburg Mosque, Maiolica of portal, in the form of Muqarnas', August 2011; photograph by CANES, used according to licensing information provided at https://creativecommons.org/licenses/by-sa/3.0/deed.en

122, 126–27, 132 MOSELLE N SINGH, hand drawn geometric illustrations provided by Moselle N Singh; used with permission.

139 Iranian glazed ceramic tile work from the ceiling of the tomb of Hafez in Shiraz, Iran, Province of Fars. Photograph by Pentocelo, 2008; public domain.

140, 150–51, 169 LUCAS CRANACH THE YOUNGER (1515–1586), 'Adam and Eve', Gemäldegalerie Alte Meister, Dresden, Germany; public domain.

170 ELISABET YANAGISAWA, detail from sketchbook; used with permission.

202, 228–29, 243 HASEGAWA TOHAKU (1539–1610), 'Pine Trees' (pair of six-folded screens; ink on paper; left hand screen; sixteenth century), Tokyo National Museum; public domain.

223 'The Dialectic of Place as a Dialectic of Vertical and Horizontal Inter-determination' (diagram), provided by John W M Krummel; used with permission. A version of this figure originally appeared in Krummel, 'Embodied Implacement in Kūkai and Nishida', *Philosophy East and West* 65.3 (July 2015).

244 HIERONYMUS BOSCH (c. 1450–1516), 'Creation' (exterior shutters of 'The Garden of Earthly Delights', c. 1480–1490), Museo del Prado, Madrid; public domain.

www.ingramcontent.com/pod-product-compliance
Lightning Source LLC
Chambersburg PA
CBHW041956080526
44588CB00021B/2760